The Boy Who Lived

An autobiography of an autistic child who
survived the trauma of being orphaned and
transitioned into a successful adulthood

Andrew Robinson

 www.trafford.com

North America & international
toll-free: 1 888 232 4444 (USA & Canada)
phone: 250 383 6864 ✦ fax: 812 355 4082

Contents

Why I Am The Boy Who Lived

I BELIEVE HARRY POTTER is the greatest story ever told. No other story means as much to me or goes into as much detail for things that are so relevant to life today, especially mine, as Harry Potter does. Some of this has to do with because I have a lot in common with three of the characters in Rowling's book: Harry Potter, Tom Riddle, and Voldemort. Like Tom Riddle and Harry Potter, I too was an orphan. Like Tom and Harry, I too was born in a world where I was neither wanted, nor needed, nor loved. Both of them had no friends for most of their lives and they were emotionally and physically abused as children. There is no way a person that grows up in an environment like that can grow up to become normal. In a university textbook I read once, titled ABNORMAL PSYCHOLOGY, it listed a table that documented what happens to most orphans after they "age out" (are old enough to become independent of the foster care system)—99% end up either homeless, prostitutes, in prison, strung out on drugs, or dead. Only 1% or less survived without succumbing to any of these dire things. Add to that the fact that only 5% of autistics and probably no children who have had depravation dwarfism can say they survived and are successful, so what are the odds I should have survived then? Yet I survived but I should have died. Like Harry Potter, I am the boy that lived.

What made Harry immune to all the people who despised and mentally abused him, leading to rejection and abuse that would psychologically destroy the vast majority of us mere mortals? In the Harry Potter series, it was because of magic. Harry had a magical personality but in real life there is no such thing as magic . . . or is there? I too, just like Harry Potter, I too went through the same torture and abuse and survived, but what was Harry's (or my) secret? I know the secret and will share it with whoever wants to listen. You don't have to believe me, just like you don't have to believe in magic, but in the end, what else can you explain it with?

My secret is very much the same as Harry Potter's: I had a magical curse placed upon me. This curse had the potential to ruin my life—and it did ruin my life—but at the same time, it is the very thing that saved my life in the end. My curse was autism.

Think about what gave Harry Potter his deep connection with Tom Riddle. Dumbledore said it was not their abilities (or similarities) that mattered, but their choices. What "choices" was Dumbledore speaking about? A better word here than "choices" would be "decisions". I would rather base my decisions; my philosophies in life, by the things I love, respect, and admire rather than the things I hate, fear, or despise. So . . .

Harry hated, feared, and despised evil. Yet Harry did not act on his hate or fear and try to suppress or repress all that was evil, but rather he looked to his friends for support and comfort from evil. Harry was even willing go so far as to die for his beliefs, even if that death accomplished nothing good in return other than giving evil one less reason to exist with him out of the picture. Harry acted like the things that happened to him were just the way things were; that this was his lot in life and he had no choice but to accept it. He went with the flow and after suffering the consequences of others actions, picked himself up, and moved on.

Tom Riddle knew that life wasn't supposed to be this way; that life wasn't supposed to be terrible. Tom felt that part of the problem must be all the supposedly good people in his life in the orphanage were holding him back from living life as it should be. So Tom acted on his hate, fear, and disgust of the supposedly good people in his life and tried to suppress and repress all that appeared good in the world. Tom was a one man show, like the hero is often portrayed as, and he used intimidation and coercion to recruit "friends" to help him fight Good. Tom was not willing to ever die and wanted to live forever. Tom Riddle was like a salmon going against the current. He fought and resisted to the end.

And Tom grew up to become a bully while Harry became the bullied.

You might think that Tom Riddle and Voldemort were the same character, but that is not quite true. Tom didn't want to be who he was and where he came from; he wanted to be someone else. Tom hated his life and left it to become someone else, an alter persona that would be everything he thought he could never be: the greatest wizard in the world. Yet paradoxically, Tom Riddle never realized that he had it in him all along to become the greatest wizard in the world anyway, he only deluded himself into believing he was being held back by others.

We can all become a Harry Potter or a Voldemort, if we are also willing to suffer the same things they had to suffer through while growing up. While a lot of people wish they were like Harry Potter, none of them are willing to suffer as much as he did to become what he was, but what he suffered is what made him into the Harry Potter we know. Yet that same suffering can backfire and lead you down the wrong path, as it did for Voldemort. Just remember this: although Voldemort is portrayed as a very evil figure, Voldemort always had the option to redeem himself, if only he would have had a change of heart ("try for some remorse", as Harry put it).

> Anyone can be broken—don't let anyone delude or deceive you. And being broken is always traumatic. No one can "tough it out" or come out unscathed. There are no "picking up the pieces" and continuing on. Every time you are truly broken, you lose something—it can be a hope or a feeling of security—but whatever it is, it is lost forever. I have been broken so many times that there is no hope that I can ever be completely whole again. It is like I have been through a devastating F6 tornado and had to crawl my way back to civilization afterwards. I've been crawling ever since. There are no heroes were I come from and there never will be any heroes. Heroes are for the movies and not real life.

MacLaren Hall

S EPT 6TH, 1960: My birthdate. I was born in Duarte, California to Constance and Douglas J Robinson. My father was an aeronautical engineer at JPL (Jet Propulsion Laboratories). I believe my mother was a court reporter (she took shorthand notes of court proceedings). They had six other kids (in order of descending age): Michael, Patrick, Dennis, Mary, Theresa, and John. I was the third youngest of the bunch. Both grandparents lived in the L.A. (Los Angeles) county area, the same as my parents.

I have no idea how old I was for any of my memories for my early years as a toddler, but I do pretty much remember the sequence of events, so that is how these early memories are portrayed. All I can say is that they occurred between the time I was born until the time I was 2 years old . . .

I was a baby and my mother was putting me away in my crib. As I lay in my crib, I saw search lights outside my window. I could not think very much in three dimensions so as far as I was concerned, the search lights were ON the window and not far away. I expressed fear to my mother by crying and then looking out the window and she told me not to be scared, but I remained scared until she closed the curtains.

As I started growing up, one day I remember climbing up on the kitchen counter and finding a can of Hershey's chocolate syrup and a butter-dish with some butter in it. I drank what was left of the chocolate syrup and then started eating away at the butter. By the time my parents discovered what I was doing, it was too late. I got very sick, mostly from eating so much butter I suspect. They seemed happy to see me sick and I couldn't understand why they felt that way towards me and it made me upset that they would feel that way.

My parents made me go outside by myself. I was in the front yard and it was a windy autumn day. I was very uncomfortable being outside by myself. As the wind blew, one particular leaf fell off the tree in the front yard and headed towards me. I panicked and was scared to death. Although I say this was a leaf now, I didn't know it was a leaf then. This memory lasted many, many years before I figured out what happened. When I was in elementary school I used to sketch a copy of this "leaf" in any of the drawings I did which included the sky as a background (which meant pretty much every single drawing I did). My teachers would ask what that thing was and I couldn't tell them. It wasn't until I was in my early 20s and working at Advanced Diagnostic Research as an electronic assembler that a woman explained to me what I probably saw—a falling leaf. All of a sudden I recognized and knew what it was.

My family went to the beach and it was my first time ever. I didn't know how to swim but that didn't stop me from going out into the water and playing a game, which in hindsight I would call "When the waves come in, lie down in the water so that you disappear and scare the death out of your family as they scramble around trying to find you". I was never scared and I never thought about what would happen if my family didn't find me and I had to breathe.

I was in the hospital to get my appendix removed. They had placed me in a room in a crib. There were other children in other cribs here too. I didn't want to be there so I pulled up the mattress and reached down through the wire grating that held the mattress up and pushed and pulled my hand through it until my plastic ID bracelet came off. I then climbed up over the crib and walked out to the elevator. I was waiting there when a black man (the janitor?) came up to me and asked what I was doing all alone there. I told him I was waiting for my mommy and daddy. He asked if I didn't mind him waiting with me and I said no. He waited anyways. The elevator came and emptied out and I went to go inside and this black man stopped me. I started crying and people started arguing. The elevator came and went and again it emptied out and this black man stopped me from leaving. Finally some hospital staff came by and took me away back to my room and put a new ID bracelet on me.

I was sitting in a kitchen. I do not know whose kitchen this was (my father's/mother's grandmother?). I could see outside and that it was raining. I was eating split-pea soup and got sick and vomited it up. The person taking caring of me seemed to get upset and picked me up, carried me through the living room and into a den and placed me in a crib. She gave me a bottle and I remember being very happy drinking this warm, sweet milk.

Sometime in 1961: The details I give here are what I gleaned from my real father when I was allowed to meet him a few months before I turned 18 ("aged out") of the California welfare system in 1978. My ≈31 year old father had an awful accident. He was on a big Harley Davidson motorcycle doing 70 MPH in downtown LA, when some woman pulled out in front of him. My father flew over the car, displacing the car over ten feet from the initial impact. Incredibly, my father survived. Unfortunately my mother didn't. She decided to file for divorce in absentia. You see, my father was comatose in a hospital for almost six months or longer. His $30,000 (in 1960 dollars) a year job was forfeited by his employers. Creditors claimed the house and furniture. My Mother's mother died in a fire. Finally, the State of California claimed the family itself. My father emerged from the hospital with "nothing" except $500,000 from a lawsuit.

I had a dream at this time of my life which scared me to death. I was lying in my crib and I saw the roof of my room fly straight up and spin away into the sky and disappear. I have no idea why that would scare me as a child because it doesn't seem very scary to me today.

Sometime in 1962: This would make me about two years old or so. I remember being driven away by a social worker while my mother remained behind. I screamed and cried. I watched my mother shrink in size to a little dot and then disappear as the car drove down the street. I was now officially an orphan; a ward of the State of California. I have no idea what happened to the rest of my family at this point, although my father told me that he took in the two oldest brothers' (Patrick and Michael) until they turned 18.

MacLaren Hall. The very first thing I remember are the locked gates that could only be opened remotely before cars could enter. It was like a prison. Next, I remember the vestibule at the entrance. Smack in the middle of the ceiling of this room was a stained glass window. This was unusual architecture to me that I had never seen before. My sister, Mary, showed up a little later at this same orphanage. Mary was one year older than I was.

I still wanted to be picked up and held by an adult but none of the adults in the orphanage would touch me or any of the many other toddlers that were here. The first person I came across who would touch me or pick me up was one of the black women who washed the children every night. I had been watching her and she had a routine where she picked up and held one of the children while she grabbed another child by the hand and led them into the wash room. So I waited for her to come out and get some more children. It was a hit and miss proposition. She picked up some other child before me and then grabbed me by my hand so I had to escape until I got what I wanted. And I did. She picked me up and held me while I hugged her in return. She then put me in the sink to wash me and I wouldn't let go. When she finally got me into the sink, I cried to this one black woman and asked if she wanted to be my mommy. All the other black women

If you take a glass jar and throw it down on the ground as hard as you can, pieces will go flying everywhere. Then if you try and put it back together again, you find that the jar won't stay together by itself anymore. If you want the jar to stay together, you need to bind the pieces back together again with glue. It is the same thing with us humans but the only glue we have to use is a woman's love. Only women can do this; only women have the healing touch. It's because women who are true to their nature are by nature nurturing, affectionate, accepting, and understanding. Men can't do this. It's not in their nature. They can't even fake it.

The world needs women and their healing touch now more than ever but it's still a man's world and there is still no room for women. Even our religions are male based with women taking second place in everything, as if it was their fault, their sin, to be born a woman. Women are still treated like second-class citizens, even here in America. I see a horrible trend in the media where men are trying to portray women as alternate versions of men. The women of movies today aren't the "overly-emotional" and "over-nurturing" people we have come to know, they are being portrayed as violent, one-man superheroes with muscles like a man's. I cannot imagine why any women would want to be like a man. Our true national treasure is the hearts of all women who are true to their nature.

After all I have been through, some people think I am strong, but I am not, I have never been strong. Instead, I find strength in women. When I have been completely broken, as I have many times in my life, if I can just hold it together until I can find a woman true to her nature, she can help put me back together again, even if I am permanently missing a few pieces, as is most often the case every time I have been broken in my life.

"Being deeply loved by someone gives you strength, while loving someone deeply gives you courage." Lao Tzu suddenly stopped what they were doing and turned to stare at me. Then the woman giving me my bath responded. She said she would get in trouble if she hugged me so she taught me how to "steal hugs" from her every time she picked me up to put me into or take me out of the sink that I was being washed in.

Do you know what effect that had on me? I have a hole in my heart the shape of a black woman. She's my mother archetype. I never forgot that. It kept me going. It gave me hope. I was very happy in the orphanage as long as she was there. I learned over time that this is what women can do and men cannot. I was very lucky to meet a woman like her when I did.

One day the black woman brought her relatives over and told me she was going to take me home. I got in the middle of the back seat of a small four door car and two adults got in on either side of me so I could hide between them. But then they all got back out because it apparently was just a test and I started squealing and crying. My "mother" told everyone to leave now and they all left. My "mother" told me she was going to get in big trouble and that she had to do something "bad" by making me look dirty. She put mud or something on my face and clothes. She said I had to cry or she would be in big trouble because the whole place had heard me and knew I was in an off-limits area. Crying was easy as all I had to do was think about how much I didn't want to be there.

The first day I had to have a bath by a different black woman, I had a temper tantrum and defecated in the water and splashed water everywhere. My "mother" came in and told me to settle down and say I was sorry so I immediately calmed down and told the other woman I was sorry and tried to help her clean up. I even went so far to scoop up my own feces and put them aside. This other woman told me not to worry about it. I could see tears in her eyes but didn't understand what they meant. I only knew crying the same way I cried: out loud and with copious tears. This kind of "crying" was different.

My houseparent (her boss?) would come into the room and say things that I cannot remember, probably because I didn't understand what he was saying. All I knew is that it was something bad. I asked my "mother" why he was like that and she told me that he was a mean person. From then on, whenever I was being given a bath and that man walked in, I would splash water all over him and make him run away.

My houseparent, a man, was unhappy that I wasn't eating. So he got angry and raised his voice and slammed his fist on the table. I certainly didn't want to eat then so I refused to eat and started crying. He then sent me to the timeout room, which I gladly obliged to do when I saw what it was: a small room with a cot to sleep on and nothing more. But I would be all alone away from all the kids and the adults. It was perfect. When the houseparent came into the time out room with a tray of food on it, I dumped the tray over onto the floor. Obviously this got him very angry again and he left, only to return sometime later with another tray. He calmly asked me to not overturn the tray and please eat something. It was the first time I heard him talk politely to me, but as soon as the tray was within reach, I dumped the tray over onto the floor. Now things were getting serious, so shortly thereafter, a different person came in—he must have been a psychologist or psychiatrist—and he talked to me real nice and listened to what I had to say and then he politely asked me if I would eat something, to which I responded with a yes. Then something terrible happened—they took me away out of the timeout room. I didn't get to spend the night there like they promised.

Thereafter I went to see that psychologist on a regular basis, about once a week. He once told me that he cared for me and was concerned for me, so I called him a liar because he wasn't there when I really needed him throughout the day. I was here and he was somewhere else and he only had to be there with me half-an-hour once-a-week or whenever it was he had to see me. If he really cared for me or was concerned for me, why didn't he take

Men act like they are the Universe's grand fix-it-uppers. Nothing is beyond their imagined ability to know and conquer. They will even give answers to problems that they know absolutely nothing about. A man's answer to any emotional problem? Turn off the emotion; emotions are bad; they are what will kill you. In our current world, men send other men to war and bring them back "broken", i.e.—suicidal, drug addicts, or have PTSD. Men compete with other men in business and send them home, broke(n). A man's idea of fixing anything that they know nothing about it is to throw 10,000 things at it and see what sticks. And if something does stick, they say, "I fixed it", and since they "fixed it", they must understand it as well. You can't reason with people like that. Men actually are good at fixing some things but they are completely incompetent when it comes to fixing things that really matter. And a man's answer to autism? Don't use autism as an excuse for your behavior. What the . . . ?! Don't act like you are autistic? What an ignorant answer.

me home with him instead of leaving me all alone? How can you say you like somebody or love somebody when you will never see them when you really needed them? I wanted to be liked or loved, not "be well", besides, how could I ever "be well" when I wasn't even liked? I eventually learned that psychology was often abused by manipulating people to act in ways that didn't upset anyone: "Eat your peas, shut up and sit down, and never complain".

My Sisters. I went to live with my real sisters, Mary and Theresa. I remember playing with a Slinky all the time, a pogo-stick horse, and in a little blow up pool. I could never figure out how to make the slinky go down the stairs the same way it would in the commercials. At some point, that foster mom decided she didn't want me anymore. She kept my sisters though.

Maybe I should elaborate on that last claim. How do I know she didn't want me anymore? Because I clearly remember the day she got rid of me. She was talking to my social worker and I had to go to the bathroom real bad and neither one would pay attention to me. It was one of those "go away kid, you bother me" kind of things. Well I just couldn't hold it back anymore. I went into the bathroom and burst—I pissed all over everything in that bathroom. I mean everything. I finally managed to come to my senses and aim for the toilet but the damage was done. Then right on cue, both of them called out for me to "come here". The next thing I knew, my foster mother came out of the bathroom, angry. She said I should be very glad that I was going away with the social worker just then because she would have let me have it. That painful remark has been stuck in my brain and my mind forever. See kept my sisters while she got rid of me. The good thing was . . .

I went to live with my real mother. She lived all alone in a small one room apartment. I slept with my mother. It is the earliest time I can definitely remember that I wet my bed. She had some kind of job where she would come home with these little square bottles that were defective. I had a whole bag of them and even though I didn't like them, I liked the fact that they were from my mother so I cherished them for that fact. I also had a little metal bandage box full of pennies from my mother that I had to carry with me where ever I went.

One day I saw my mother on the phone crying very loudly. I had an easel she bought me and I used it to draw things on. So to try and comfort my mother, I started drawing all different kinds of animals on different sheets of paper and giving them to her to try and make her feel better. She said she "didn't have the money" to whoever she was talking to on the phone. Next thing I remember in this memory segment was I was waiting outside for the social worker to come and pick me up. I had scuffed my finger against the wall of the house while playing in the dirt and my mother put some iodine on my finger and wrapped a bandage around it. I revered that bandage for a long time afterward and didn't want to ever take it off. I can't remember if the social worker ever came to pick me up. I think she showed up but she left without me. Now the next thing I remember was my mother abandoning me in front of (what I believe was) the Department of Economic Security. My mother told me to "wait here" and she would "be right back". I started crying when she left and she came back to comfort me. She told me everything was okay and just wait here. She left and (what I believe was) one of my real brothers came over and talked to me. Then he left. I was then taken inside the building and my "world", as it existed in my toddler mind then, consisted of a hallway connected to the room I was in. A man was doing paperwork in this room when he had to leave. He told me to "wait here" but I didn't wait and took off a short way down a hallway to get a drink of water, as I was thirsty from all the crying I had been doing. I couldn't reach the water fountain so I waited for adults to walk by while I stood by the water fountain and whined. I did this for quite some time until finally I had my fill but now I couldn't tell where the social worker's office was so I did the only thing I knew how to do back then: I started crying. It wasn't long until some adults came out and calmed me down and found my social worker. Boy was he mad too.

Another home. I remember having bad ear infections at this home. One day these foster parents forced me to go outside and play by myself for some reason. I know I was obsessed with The Lone Ranger and they didn't seem pleased by that. I

> It used to be children would play games of make believe and pretending; now they use computer games to do the pretending for them. People used to talk at the table—now they just text everyone except each other.

was out in the front yard just standing there and they were asking me why I didn't play. I didn't know how to play with "nothing". They told me to pretend. Pretend what? Then they said I could be the Lone Ranger and pretend that I was saving the world. Suddenly I knew what to do and I fell to the ground and played dead. I scared the hell out of these foster parents when I did that and they started screaming at me and asking if I was okay. So I yelled back and told them that I was attacked and hurt badly but that Tonto would be by in a little bit and rescue me, just like he did on TV. This experienced opened up a whole new world to me of using my imagination. I could do things in my mind that otherwise would not be permitted or would be impossible.

These foster parents were Catholics. At the Cathedral they frequented, there were these half-bowls filled with water attached to the walls and certain people would put their hands in them and do funny things with it that I didn't understand. So one day I went up and started playing and splashing in all the water bowls, as another kid had taught me to do. I loved the crackers and grape juice they served too. All I remember next is the Priest being angry with me and taking me aside with my foster parents and saying something bad about me.

The other children in the family used to go on walks, I think to school and to a park. All I can remember is how we got there and not where we went. One of the things the kids did when going for a walk was jaywalk. They would stand on the curb and look both directions. They would wait for cars to pass and then cross. Sometimes we had to run. And sometimes they would go halfway and then wait for a car to pass before crossing the rest of the way. So one day I was out in the front yard playing all by myself again when I thought it would be a good idea to practice crossing the street by myself. I followed the same protocol but the drivers weren't acting like they normally would when I was with the other kids. They were staring and honking at me. Finally I tried crossing the road halfway and waiting for a car to pass by before crossing the rest of the way. Wouldn't you know it, the old folks driving that car didn't pass by, instead they stopped and laid on the horn without stopping. It was a horrible loud noise, but I didn't move. I still waited for them to pass by. Then my foster parents came to the kitchen window and started yelling at me. The old folks stopped honking their horn. The foster parents asked what I was doing and I said I was practicing crossing the road as the rest of us had done many times before. I tried waving the old folks on by but they still wouldn't budge. The foster parents told me to get in the house right now, so I started to finish crossing the road and as I was crossing, I ran my hand across the hood of the old folk's car. The old folks honked their horn at me and that pissed me off because I didn't like sudden loud noises so as I finished crossing the street, I slapped the top of the hood of their car as hard as I could as I walked along. Later on the foster parents asked why I was slapping the hood of the car and I told them because I didn't like the sound of the horn.

I was at some kind of classroom with other kids. We were all drawing and then the teacher left the room. One of the kids started some trouble by scribbling on my drawing. I went over and scribbled back on his drawing. We did this back and forth for a little while when the other kids started complaining, so this other kid started scribbling on their drawings too. Soon other kids were scribbling on other kids drawings. Pandemonium ensued. Then the teacher was coming back. All the kids sat back down . . . except for me. I was the only one who got caught and got in trouble.

I remember still seeing my real mother while at this home. One time I went to see a doctor and my mom and the doctor had to hold me down while the doctor pricked my foot with a needle in order to get something out of it. My foot had a sharp recurring pain there until I was in my early 40's when it just disappeared for no reason. I believe today that this was a symptom of my MS (Multiple Sclerosis). My mother took me to a restaurant afterward.

One day these foster parents sat me down in the kitchen and read a story to me. It was about the angel Gabriel I think. After they read me the story, I got up, walked through the first bedroom connected closest to the kitchen where the kids were playing a game of cards, and I walked all over the cards and scattered them around. This made my foster parents extremely angry. They took me to the center of the house and made me stand against the wall where the whole family could see me. Then they yelled at me and asked why I would do what I did. These people thought I was demon possessed so they sent me away.

Another home. One day, someone dropped a glass in the kitchen—probably me. There were fragments everywhere. I was amazed at how everyone in the family reacted to things like that.

They were all very scared and told me not to move, but I got tired of standing still so I moved anyways. Of course, I cut my foot on some glass and now the fear turned into anger. I could not understand either reaction.

I want to stop here and remind you to realize that children do not think like adults. They do not reason like adults. They think like a separate species. Take child abuse for example. As an abandoned child, I had a chronic lack of appetite. I believe I was on the verge of failing to thrive at this home. So I was very underweight and my current foster parents were concerned. They tried to force me to eat. Then one night, once again I (truthfully) said I wasn't hungry. We were having Chow Mein that night and I said I felt sick. It was something new that we hadn't had for dinner before. The father thought I was faking and well "enough was enough" and the father sent me to my room, had me undress to my underwear and had me sleep in the bathtub, where "'sick' children should sleep". As any three or four year old would do, I whined and cried until the father told me he was going to give me something to cry about. I was miserable and very cold and, of course, sick. I woke up in the middle of the night to throw up. Of course I made a big fuss and started crying and the father yelled at me from his room for me to shut up. My foster mom came into the bathroom and took me out. I remember bright lights and then a blanket. I was warm and happy then and that was all I knew. That is, until someone, maybe one of the other foster kids, told my social worker what happened, and then all hell broke loose. Bunches of people came into the house, packed all our belongings, and took me and all the other foster kids away. I didn't understand this. I told the social worker that I didn't want to be with the "meanie" father, but the mother was okay and I could stay with just her. I had no concept of child abuse then and it took me many years to realize exactly what had happened on a deeper level than what I had thought happened as a child.

This home gave me what became one of most favorite toys: a cement truck made out of rubber.

Back to MacLaren Hall again. At night, once a week, the kids would be gathered together and pick gifts off of a table. The houseparent picked me because I was new. The table had all kinds of toys on it, as well as a small black and white TV Set. I could pick

ANYTHING I wanted, and while I can't remember exactly what it was I picked, I didn't pick the TV set and that made me very unpopular. Then for some strange reason, the houseparent told me to pick again. This time I listened to the kids who were the loudest and most uniform in their requests, and I picked the TV. I went and sat back down by my roommates at their bench and they were picking on me, physically. That's when a few (older) kids from the other bench came over and sat by me and defended me. I had just inadvertently learned the value—not of making friends—but of gaining other people's respect and gratitude by being considerate of their feelings. I learned this after I went back to my section of the wing and discovered that the toy that I had picked out wasn't just for me, but for my roommates within that particular wing, and the TV was for a different group of (older) kids. So that is why the older kids defended me!

Yet I couldn't keep my new toy and neither could I keep my old toy cement truck. I was devastated. I didn't want to give them up and my roommates got even angrier with me than they already were. I would lose that battle obviously and sure enough, the next day, I found my toy cement truck—broken in half. Some of the adults seemed concerned that I had absolutely no desire to line up with the other kids to get toys out of the toy box. With no toys to call my own and the ones I had the opportunity to play with not being desirable, I played with the one thing I could call my own: my imagination. The imaginary people I played with were an ancient culture and wore long flowing robes. The men in my imaginary world all had long white beards, just like they did in the stories that the Catholic family used to read to me.

I wanted to get out of that place so badly that I devised a plan. On my way into the orphanage, we had driven under an overpass and I saw a drain pipe outlet at the bottom of the bridge superstructure. At the back of the orphanage where we were supposed to play, I saw a pipe in the ground for storm water drainage, and I knew that it was the same pipe that I saw on my way in. I was barely big enough to fit inside of it but I did fit inside and I crawled I don't know how many feet before discovering that it wasn't a straight pipe. So I backed out because I didn't want to get stuck. Another bigger kid had seen me do this and told me to go back inside and I said no, so he got another kid and made him crawl inside. That kid got stuck with only his feet showing. They had to chip at the cement and break open the ceramic pipe to get the child out. They then repaired the drain with cement and covered the opening over with chicken wire.

At MacLaren Hall, every day they had roll call in which the children would all line up in front of the houseparent, and the houseparent would call out each child's name and the child would respond and receive a piece of candy. Well I didn't want to be there so I decided that when my name was called, I wouldn't respond—the same thing that would happen if I really wasn't there. So the houseparent called out my name and I didn't respond. Again the houseparent called my name and again I didn't respond. He yelled out my name. Silence. Has anyone seen Andrew Robinson? Does anyone know where Andrew Robinson is? Oh, there he is! Why didn't you speak up when I called your name as you were told to do? So the houseparent took me aside and made me face the wall as punishment. I cried and cried, which only made the houseparent angrier, so after roll call he yelled at me and asked why didn't I speak up when he called my name and I cried out, because I didn't want to be there and that made me feel I wasn't there. I thought that they would think, "Oh, here is an extra child that doesn't belong here, so let him go free". Somehow he must have understood my thoughts so he brought me a handful of candy and told me I was free to go.

One thing I learned at the orphanage was that I loved school. School was structured

I have often been labeled a "late bloomer". That means that when I was learning something new in school, I would academically be way behind everyone else in class until towards the end of the class, then all of a sudden I would catch up or zoom way ahead of everyone else. Now this statement needs clarification. Having autism meant that I was easily confused when first presented with new information, especially if it was only partial information. Non-Autistics are illogical and unorganized by nature, so their approach to learning will also be illogical and unorganized. They will haphazardly throw facts out with no explanation behind them, and expect you to use and memorize them at face value. It is only later, often times much later, during the course of learning things that they will finally explain the principles behind the facts. As an Autistic, my tendency was NOT to remember reams of facts UNLESS they were USEFUL. This is the result of another key trait of Autistics: they are very practical-minded. Getting good grades in a class is not useful, no matter how much they lie to us and try to tell us that they are. Now if it isn't cool or inspiring or has some utility in my immediate life, then forget it, I don't want to know.

and everyone had routines that everyone followed. Kids couldn't do whatever they wanted to do, so school was a calm and peaceful place to be. It was my favorite time all during the week. I always did very well in school clear up until I turned 18. I was an honor roll student and took classes that other students didn't or couldn't take like Trigonometry.

Another home. There was a kid here (a neighbor?) who liked to play with fire. When we were playing in the backyard at the side of the house one day, he started lighting all the dead stalks of grass on fire. He would then comment on how beautiful fire looked. I told him that yes, fire is beautiful to watch but fire was also dangerous. So I went around putting out his little fires that he had started. This upset him and I think he never forgave me for that. Later on we were at what I think was a PTA meeting at a school. There were lots of adults standing around talking and this same kid came over to me and told me to hold a lighter up to a curtain. I didn't want to and I can't remember whether I gave in to his request or not or whether he started the curtains on fire himself, but he told me to stay there and don't move. He took off and I watched as the curtains caught up in flames. An adult came over and took me away. The building was evacuated and as we were driving off, the police stopped us and questioned me about the fire. I told them that some kid, whose name I didn't know, had started the fire and then made me stay and watch it. Apparently they didn't believe me and I must have been under observation of some kind because I remember one of my social workers apologizing to me about thinking that I had started that fire, that they know now that I had been telling the truth because that same kid I met at this foster home had started a fire at another home and it burned down and killed the parents.

My foster brother was mean. He constantly tried to scare me about a horrible monster living under my bed inside the mattress—a booger bear. Actually his plan to scare me worked very well and I remained scared of the dark and of a monster living under my bed until I was in my early 40's. It took me that long to realize the ridiculousness of such a concept.

I remember eating Spaghetti O's and loving them to the exclusion of anything else. I went to the backyard and analyzed things, like how a chain hung down when draped between two poles. The shape that it had was a parabola.

There was a Christmas tree in the backyard one day and I tried to walk up as close as I could to it and I got stabbed by a sharp branch on it. Where it had stabbed me turned into a mole.

I had a piece of long string which I played with. One of the things I did constantly was put it up my nose. My foster parents would scold me for doing it but I kept doing it until one day I stuffed it so far up my nose I couldn't get it out. I started crying and as I was crying the string started coming out and gave me a bloody nose. My foster parents were furious at me.

It was easy for me to get lost and I was always getting lost because I was always wandering off. I remember wandering out into the street one day, turned around and realized that I couldn't determine which of the many houses on the street were mine. I could tell you the architectural layout of the house, even to this day, but I couldn't use that information to tell "my house" from someone else's house.

While being "interviewed" for another home, I got into trouble. Seems the kid that lived there didn't like the way I played. He tried to get me to play the way he wanted me to play and I didn't want to. I finally got tired of his game so when he crawled into his toy box to get some more toys, I closed the lid on him. His mother quickly found out what I had done and said I was not welcomed there and to leave.

The Decent's

Sometime in 1965: Josephine & Cecil H Decent. I was about 4-1/2 years old.

My social worker and my new mom had to carry me inside while I kicked and screamed and begged not to stay there. My new parents were actually old parents—in their early 60's. They had all kinds of animals on their three acre farm. They had everything from skunks to geese to cats.

My relationship with Cecil did not begin very well. Once again, I still had no appetite and refused to eat very much. One night we were eating spaghetti and meatballs but I wasn't eating enough to their satisfaction, so Cecil took some noodles and put ketchup in it instead of spaghetti sauce. I took a few enthusiastic bites (it was very sweet) but I just as quickly lost my appetite. Cecil screamed and yelled at me until I cried and then forced me to eat the entire cup of noodles. Eating together at the table was not one of my most favorite times of the day. Cecil thought that by yelling at me and telling me to eat, he would get me to eat more. Well that was stupid and very typical. I had no will to thrive; there was nothing for me to live for so do you think that I would have more of a will to live if you yelled at me? Hello! Get a clue, folks! Yelling is the language of hate, not love, and demonstrating hate towards someone who doesn't want to live in the first place is not going to make them want to live more. It certainly won't make them want to eat more food; at best it will only force them to eat only while you are around. When you are not around, things will go back to the way they were or worse; the way things should have been without you.

The Decent's loved to drink alcohol. Every day they would have me take a sip of a Hot Toddy. I did not like the taste of alcohol but I did it because they made me. And because they loved to drink, every Christmas, Josephine would get so drunk that she couldn't get out of her chair and would throw up. This scared me because when I saw this I thought she was dying.

Because I wet my bed, Cecil continually called me "piss pot" or "piss ant"—and if that didn't make me feel wanted, what would? Anytime Cecil got up at night, he would wake me up and make me go to the bathroom. Obviously, Cecil did not like me.

I loved to take my Tonka Toys apart and put them back together again, but Tonka Toys were supposed to be "indestructible" so when Cecil came outside one day and saw how I once again completely disassembled my Tonka Trucks into individual pieces, he took all the Tonka toys away from me for good. I cried and explained that they weren't broken and that they could easily be put back together again, but he wouldn't listen and I could do nothing about it. No matter, I learned to play without them.

I still absolutely loved school. All my childhood life, I spent more time at school then I did at home. I would even go so far as to say that my real childhood homes were my schools. I loved studying and reading. I was a reading expert and was way ahead of the other kids in reading comprehension. I didn't love recess but I did love hanging out at the library at recess or lunch. Even the walk to school was fascinating. People would put their trash out on the curb and one day someone put an old TV set on the curb. I explored this TV set in exquisite detail before figuring out that there were very strong magnets on the yoke of the CRT. I tried taking them off but I couldn't until a man came outside with a screwdriver and helped me remove the magnets and I took them home with me.

That doesn't mean I didn't have problems at school though. For one thing, I didn't play with the other kids because I couldn't make sense of what they were doing and saying when they played. For example, the teacher had all the kids from our class get together to learn to play volleyball. The teacher told me to stand at the back of the court and try to hit the ball when it comes over the net. So I took my place at the back of the court and every time the ball came over the net, I would run around trying to hit it. "No Andrew, stand at the back of the court and don't move from that spot". So I took my place at the back of the court again and watched a ball bounce beside me without doing anything. The teacher wondered why I didn't hit the ball and I said because she told me to stand and not move from that spot. No, you have an imaginary area all around where I was standing where I could move and hit the ball back only whenever it came into my imaginary area. So once again I took my place at the back of the court and eventually the volleyball came to a girl in front of me and she missed and it landed in my area. Why wasn't I hitting the ball? Of course because it didn't come to my area, it came into the girl's area first—it was her ball and she missed it, not me. No Andrew, you need to watch the volleyball and wait to hit any balls that anyone might miss, even if they weren't in your area. So I took my place at the back of the court and ran around the court, following the ball around and standing behind anyone that might miss the ball . . . well you get the point. The kids were yelling at me and I'm sure the teacher probably thought I was being difficult on purpose. I was never a popular kid for other to kids to play with on the playground, but I didn't care because being alone at the library was my favorite place to be at recess or lunch anyway.

During one of our classes, they played a Hawaiian song. Having seen a documentary on Hula dancers on TV, I knew how the dance was supposed to be done so when one day the teacher asked us to stand up and dance, the kids went crazy with the way I danced. Thereafter, every time they played that Hawaiian song, the kids would beg me to stand up and dance for them—which I gladly did. I was never embarrassed to do this until some of the other kids started talking to me afterward and telling me how ridiculous or stupid I looked doing it. Actually their comments made me feel bad but I continued with my behavior anyways, thinking I was doing it only for the kids that actually wanted to see me dance and didn't think I looked stupid doing it.

There were bullies at school too. These older kids would take the large, dark green, empty 10-gallon trashcans, tip them over and place them over younger kids in the school corridors. They would then force the younger kids to stay imprisoned by the trashcan until the kid stopped putting up a fight, and then they would walk away and leave the kid trapped until an adult came by and set them free. Many a bullied kid had to be sent to the nurse after this, as some of them became overheated or nearly suffocated to death. I had this happen a couple of times before I learned (by watching others get bullied) that if I didn't put up a fight and just waited a few minutes, I could just simply turn the trashcan over and be free, as the bullies would have walked away by then. I also learned to thwart their schemes by taking the trashcan away, whenever I saw it in the corridor. Also, whenever I saw the trashcan sitting upside-down in the middle of the school corridors, I knew this could only mean one thing and I would tip them over and free the bullied kids. The bullies hated me for this.

Another thing the bullies would do is hit kids in the stomach as they were leaving the school grounds, right after school was let out. When Josephine saw this happen to me one day, she decided I was wimpy and needed some muscle to help defend myself, so she forced me to stand in the front yard while holding small weights in my hands and doing various exercises while she talked on the phone. She told me to defend myself and hit back when bullies bothered me. This kind of backfired one day when another kid almost my same age, was making fun of me as I walked onto the school grounds at the beginning of the day. He didn't really hit me or anything, but he was in-my-face and mocking me, so I took the Bozo The Clown lunch pail I was carrying and did a pirouette which brought the lunch pail around with me and hit him upside the back of his head. He cried copiously and never ever picked on me again after that, but unfortunately, Josephine, who had dropped me off at school that morning in her brown Oldsmobile, saw what I did and she was furious at me.

During recess, a kid taught me how to lift dresses on girls, so I went around lifting dresses on the girls and making them scream or cry. Strangely enough, some of the girls didn't seem to mind or even enjoyed me lifting their dresses. Of course, I got into a lot of trouble with the principal over this behavior.

One day we came back from a short summer vacation and the first thing I had to do was give the pet dogs a fresh bowl of food, but before I could do that I had to clean out the old rotten dog food first. It was Purina Dog Chow and it was full of maggots. Well I found the maggots fascinating and decided to keep one as a "pet". I accomplished this feat by keeping the maggot under a bandage on my arm where I had recently gotten ringworm. Josephine was talking on the phone to a friend when she saw me playing with the maggot. She freaked out big time and I got in big trouble, even though I didn't feel I did anything wrong.

One day one of my teachers brought in a book. It was a Time book on the evolution of man and I loved it. I loved it so much that I stole it and took it home. Josephine asked about how I got such a nice book and found out I stole it, so the next day she and I went to school together and I handed the book back to my teacher.

I got a new brother. He said his name was Johnny Hollywood, although I'm not sure that was his real name. He talked about wanting to give Cecil blow jobs because his real father had made him give him blow jobs all the time. He asked if he could suck on my wee-wee and I said that wasn't right and don't talk about it. I met lots of kids in the orphanages and foster homes that had been through all kinds of strange and horrible things, so I didn't doubt he had done or would do such things.

Johnny and I never got along. When I was at school, I went to the library alone as usual but Johnny had other ideas about our relationship and went into a temper tantrum because I wouldn't play with him. Josephine insisted that I play ball with Johnny during recess because Johnny was the new kid in school and had no friends yet. So in compliance, I went to the library again, but this one time I was with a girl, and I was standing by the door to the library. Johnny complained about keeping my promise to play with him so I waited for him to throw a ball to me, which he did, and then I threw it back, saying, "Okay, now I've kept my promise and played ball with you", but before I could open the door to the library and leave Johnny alone, Johnny ran at me in a full fury of a temper tantrum. He went to hit the girl so I stood in front of her and blocked his hits. Johnny fell to the ground and screamed that I had hit him. I had to go to the Principal's office and then face the "Inquisition" when I got home that day over this incident. Johnny couldn't ever seem to do anything wrong after this incident, he had become a "Golden Boy".

I loved to play alone on the seesaw on the swing-set in the backyard. I could rock back and forth on the seesaw all day long, if I was allowed. Johnny came a little too close to the seesaw one day, and got clobbered in the mouth by the foot pegs during the upswing. This happened a few times and each time I was blamed for doing it on purpose. Then one day Johnny was on the seesaw by himself but we had some guests over and Johnny clobbered two other kids in the mouth with the seesaw, just as I had accidentally done with him, only it seemed to me that Johnny did it on purpose. Cecil came outside and asked what I had done but I happily told him that I was nowhere near the swing-set when it happened—all he had to do was ask anybody where I was at this whole time it was happening. Cecil acted as though, still, I had to have something to do with it. I remember Cecil talking about how he got in a lot trouble for that incident ("teeth-work") and he shortly went outside after that and took the seesaw apart and chained it down so it wouldn't move. I was always mystified by the fact that Cecil was apparently punishing me for something Johnny had done.

One day I tried playing with some sticks that had nails in them, even though I knew I wasn't supposed to. I threw one of the sticks and a nail in the stick caught my finger and went up inside it from the second joint to past the first joint. I couldn't pull the stick out and I didn't want to get in trouble so I went inside the house and hid my hand and the stick so Josephine couldn't see it. I went to bed and in the middle of the night I woke up and removed the stick from my hand. The next day I went to school but couldn't write because my finger was too sore and swollen. I had to go to the nurse's office and they reported it to Josephine. Surprisingly I didn't get into trouble for that.

I had heard stories about flying saucers and aliens so I started to play imagine that I was this alien scientist sent to this planet to study the humans and my home planet was Zentar. Zentar had a very large mountain located at its North Pole, a mountain so large that it could be seen from space. I believe that this reflected the fact that I have always felt alien to this world. I also had a not-so-nice fantasy in which I imagined I was a patient in some mental hospital and that I was imagining everything happening to me but the real me was "asleep" and when the real me woke up, I would be in a different world from the one I was currently in, a better world where everyone made more sense.

Johnny was taunting me one day and I let him. As he was walking around, he was looking at me standing at the opposite side of the yard from where he was and he was not paying attention to where he was going. I saw him walking towards a big spider web that had a big spider smack in the middle of it, right at eye level. As Johnny walked towards it, I said nothing and let him walk right into the spider web. Johnny immediately fell on the ground and started screaming bloody murder in a very high-pitched voice. I did nothing because I didn't want to get blamed for doing something to Johnny again as usual, but nevertheless, Cecil came outside to see what horrible thing was happening and he saw Johnny lying on the ground and me standing calmly by on the other side of the yard just watching him scream, so naturally they assumed I must have somehow been the cause of all of this or that I was enjoying watching Johnny suffer—why else wasn't I running over to help him? I just couldn't win.

One day Johnny was having one of his temper tantrums and was trying to hit me again, so I got a stick and used it to block his hits. Johnny cried bloody murder until Cecil called outside and told me to stop it and put the stick down. But Johnny, who was quiet now, went to hit me again and I also once again held up the stick and blocked it. Johnny cried bloody murder again and Cecil came outside, took my stick, and slugged me in the stomach. Johnny acted like he was happy.

Josephine used to punish me by making me stand facing a wall in the kitchen. She would then hit me and slap me in a non-abusive way but I found it very annoying so one day I eventually hit back. Josephine called Cecil and told him what happened. Cecil then proceeded to hit me and knock me to the ground. I scrambled to get back up and he would knock me down again. I would hit the cabinets and the floor, and pots and pans would come out of the cabinets and scatter all around. This happened about four times before Josephine made him stop. In hindsight, I could see that Cecil was trying to intimidate me and probably would have done some serious physical harm—if not literally kill me—if Josephine had not intervened. Josephine asked me afterward why I didn't stay down when Cecil knocked me down and I told her because it was unnatural to be lying down on the floor with the pots and pans and it would have been wrong for me to do something that didn't seem right.

The Decent's loved to travel every summer to Mexico, as Josephine was a Mexican herself, or travel to a vacation home near Joshua Tree National Park. Their favorite hobby was sport fishing, so we would go out on large ships during the Mexico trips and fish for fish so big, that even with their heads and tails cut off, they still couldn't fit into the bathtub. On one of these Mexican summer vacations, we all went out on Cecil's private boat out onto the ocean. Well Cecil didn't plan it out very well this one time, most likely because there were a lot of head winds kicking up, and he ran out of gas before he could make it back into port, but he did make it to the breakwater of the port. Unfortunately the boat was now adrift and heading for the breakwater. Cecil and Josephine had everyone take their places on the boat, with me at the very back and Johnny behind the steering wheel. We hit the rocks and I saw the steering wheel pull apart from the framing of the dashboard. Johnny was holding up the steering wheel and making steering motions while screaming bloody murder. Well I found that hysterical, with Johnny looking like he was trying to steer the boat with a steering wheel that wasn't even connected to anything. In the meantime, a sailboat happened along and threw us a rope. Well the rope missed so the sailboat made another pass and this time Cecil caught the rope. The sailboat towed us into the harbor and into safety. Thereafter I had a long sit down talk with the Decent's as they tried to desperately find out why I would find anything funny during that "frightening accident" but I couldn't explain anything to them to their satisfaction. They acted like they were scared of me.

On a trip to Joshua Tree, Josephine and I went into a tourist shop on the way over. As we walked around, I followed Josephine. There was this man and he was holding hands with his daughter, as they walked around too. I followed Josephine up to a glass counter, and as she looked at whatever was in the displays, I put my hands up on the counter. Well, remember that man and his daughter? He had walked over and with his daughter's hand in his left hand, he placed his right hand over mine. I didn't react. I looked up at him and expected him to look back at me and realize that I wasn't his child. He was talking to someone but wouldn't look at me. Then he started walking away from the counter, with my hand in his hand. I tried talking to him but he told me to be quiet. He never looked at me. As we kept walking away from the counter, Josephine cried out. The man stopped, looked at me, then looked back at Josephine with a surprised look, and then let me go. Josephine took me aside and scolded me. She said that if I ever let some man touch me and I didn't start screaming out for help, that she would kill me. And then she let me go. As I walked around, I ran into that man again, and again he took my hand into his, ever so nonchalantly, as before. He never looked at me and all the while he was talking to someone else in the store, although who that other person was I never knew because I never looked to see who he was talking to. As he started walking towards the exit, I was apprehensive, but not scared. What really scared me was what Josephine told me, so I screamed out as loud as I could for help. Everyone turned to stare at us, including Josephine. Then there was very loud arguing and angry faces everywhere. This scared me more than anything. The man said that he had lots of kids and he was always on autopilot, automatically grabbing and trying to rein in his many other children. As people started approaching him, he backed out the exit and took off.

Strangely enough, I thought for the longest time that the Decent's were the best foster parents I ever had, until suddenly it occurred to me one day that they were in fact, very bad parents, at least towards me. I didn't understand that what Cecil did, demonstrated hate and disrespect towards me until after I turned 40 years old. I also didn't understand that while all this hate and disrespect came from Cecil, Josephine didn't shield me from his hate, which means she secretly sided with him.

Sometime in 1968: **Sierra Madre.** Cecil had a stroke and I started getting frequent visits from social workers again. Heck, I probably gave Cecil the stroke for all that I know. The social workers were asking me if I was happy living there. Then one day while I was in school at Potrero Elementary School, a sudden recess was called but a bunch of people came into the room and asked me to stay behind. A social worker came and immediately drove me to another foster home. I had no time to pack any of my clothes or toys. They made it very clear that I was a gift to the foster mother's daughter to be her brother. We were almost the same age, which was about eight years old at the time.

The new foster parents wanted to make me more independent or something, so one of the things they did was make me walk to school on my own. The problem was I couldn't find my way back home. I walked around and around and the only thing I could recognize was the house of a friend of my foster sister. Finally, out of desperation, I went into my foster sister's friend's house and I was so upset, I wound up crying on her shoulder. This kind of freaked out the mom and the sister but they seemed to enjoy it at the same time.

I got in constant trouble at this new home. One of the things I got into trouble for was for my bedwetting. As a punishment for wetting my bed they made me sleep in a baby's crib with diapers on. This was very humiliating and did nothing to stop me from wetting my bed. Another punishment they decided to use was to call my foster grandmother, who turned out to be my favorite teacher from Potrero Elementary. I felt very much hated and I was unhappy. I phoned the Decent's one day and asked if they wanted me to run away and return to them. They said no, it was too late. I said what happened to Johnny and they said he was still living with them. They let me talk to him on the phone and it depressed me to hear him still living there while I was "kidnapped". Now I felt I was without any hope.

My foster parents heard me talking on the phone to the Decent's and while they questioned me about it, I received no punishment but I think they knew I was very unhappy. So when the social worker came to pick me up to take me someplace else where I could be happier, she and the foster mother were talking to each other. As I walked out the door with the social worker, the foster mother blurted out, "Why? Why didn't you like us and why don't you want to stay with us?". I told her about the bedwetting and how they embarrassed me in front of my favorite teacher. The foster mom said that she had no idea that I felt that way about her mom and that she was very sorry and that if I could ever forgive her, would I come back to stay and if I did, she promised she would fight to keep me. I stood there for a few seconds and almost said yes but I said no, and walked away. It wasn't fair for me to make that kind of decision at such a young age and I have often very much regretted making that decision. Even with the not-so-good father and the so-so sister, a loving, sensitive mother like that could have had an enormously good effect on me. I often wonder what my life would have been like if I only would have said yes that day.

The Gestalt's

SOMETIME IN 1969: TRUDY and Fred Gestalt. Covina.

I was nine years old now and on my very first day at this home, I saw Keith, one of the foster boys living there, point a BB gun at Richard, the other foster boy. We were at Sonrise Elementary School after school hours and Keith was practicing target shooting when he came across Richard playing basketball with some other kids. I told Keith he couldn't point a BB gun at Richard because guns were dangerous and you should never point them at someone, even if they were empty. Yet Keith asked me to watch him "empty" the BB gun but I couldn't tell if it really was empty or not. Keith said he was just pretend shooting. I heard Keith mumble something about hating Richards guts, then Keith pointed the BB gun at Richard again and pulled the trigger. Richard dropped to the ground and Keith ran over to him to see if Richard was okay. Richard acted like he was in a lot of pain and Keith helped Richard extract the BB from just under his collar bone. That night I told Trudy the truth about what had happened and she took the gun away and never gave it back.

I used to "swim" in a small little inflatable pool in the backyard of the Decent's house. I could float around in it and I thought this meant I knew how to swim. So when the Gestalt's asked if I knew how to swim and I told them yes, I really didn't know how to swim. I waded in the shallow area and made a few splashes and they told me to head to deeper water and show them I could swim. Well as soon as I hit the deep end, I went straight to the bottom. I kicked off the bottom to get to the surface and went down again. I kept doing this until I got enough sense to kick towards the side of the pool and grab ahold of the sides. The Gestalt's thought this was amusing. I think they probably thought I was lying about being able to swim but I really thought I could swim, I was just mistaken.

Whenever Fred was home, i.e.—he was not on travel, he would take us out every Friday to Sizzler's Steakhouse for some steak. Fred would get angry with me because I would not eat the whole steak, rather I would pick it apart so as to avoid eating any form of fat. Fred considered this the best part of the steak because fat is what gave a steak flavor. I

I was obviously very picky about what I ate while growing up—a very autistic trait. Nowadays I love fatty meats and runny eggs but I still don't like to eat vegetables in general, although I can be coaxed into eating vegetables if they are prepared in a certain way. There are a few choice vegetables that I do like to eat if they are prepared a certain way, the challenge being trying to figure out what those vegetables are and how they should be prepared. All I can suggest to parents of autistic children is to experiment with lots of different vegetables prepared in lots of different ways. For example, I hate boiled cauliflower but I love it when it is raw and dipped in salad dressing. I hate cooked carrots but I love them raw. I don't like broccoli but I will eat quite a bit of it if it is stir-fried, so that it is still crisp, and it has been soaked in the juices of some meat. In other words, experiment!

also hated eggs of any kind if they were the slightest bit runny and I wasn't very fond of eating vegetables. Once again, I had an eating problem, and this annoyed Fred to no end.

Trudy left Keith in charge of us younger kids; we had to listen to him and do what he said to do, but Keith was a bully. He would yell and call us names and hit us. One day I had had enough. Keith would randomly pick on me at all times of the day or night so I took the tweezers from a microscope set that the Decent's had bought me and hid it under my pillow. I was sound asleep and Keith came into the room, turned on the lights and started yelling about how I hadn't done one of my chores that day or something like that. So I took the tweezers and stabbed him in the hand about five times. He went to the hospital but strangely enough, I neither got a talking to nor got punished for that, but I also was never picked on again for quite a long while . . . that is until Keith's brother, Carrie, came to live with us a year or so later, then the bullying dramatically escalated only then there were two bullies.

I was very interested in books, mainly science or technical books. I loved reading the magazine, Popular Science. I saw an advertisement in Popular Science for their book club. They would give you three free books for joining their book club so I joined. Unfortunately I didn't read the fine print about having to buy a book a month thereafter or something like that, so when Fred got a call about a breach of contract, I got called by Fred. Fred was not happy paying full price for those three books.

Trudy got us up early one morning and after breakfast, had us brush our teeth with salt. I was told we were going to the dentist and I think this was the first time I had ever gone to see a dentist. When we got there, the dentist and I were alone and we talked. I had thirteen cavities and one tooth that needed a cap. He asked me what I wanted to do about it, so we discussed the various types of fillings and how long they would last and so on. I picked silver because silver had natural antibiotic properties due to its property of shedding silver ions in solution that in turn were toxic to bacteria. Naturally, this was almost the most expensive option and the dentist proceeded to do his work. When Fred was told the price at the receptionist's desk, he was angry and said something about me costing him too much money.

For the vast majority of my life, I never liked to brush my teeth, trim my fingernails, wear underarm deodorant, or sometimes even comb my hair. These actions had no practical utility, in my mind, although I would use a toothpick or chew gum after every meal. You parents out there, don't complain about your autistic children using a toothpick or chewing gum after every meal instead of brushing their teeth, it is better than nothing, so encourage your autistic children to do this. When I finally did start to brush my teeth, trim my fingernails, and wear underarm deodorant regularly, it was because I decided I wanted to "find a lover". I reasoned that I couldn't touch a woman anywhere on her body if I wasn't clean. It would be uncomfortable to her to touch her knowing my fingernails were full of bacteria and dirt.

My hair used to hurt just to be touched, all the time. I hear this is a common complaint amongst Autistics, so I would like to make a suggestion in regards to this. I find that what makes my hair hurt is the oils in my hair. These oils seem to be too thick or something. What helped me reduce this sensitivity is to 1) cut my hair really short and keep it short, or 2) when taking a shower/bath, start by soaking your hair in a lather. Don't massage the scalp or anything like that, just gently rub the shampoo into your hair, but don't rinse it out right away. Wait until the end of your shower/bath, then rinse it out and shampoo your hair one more time but in the regular fashion to complete this process. Then use some conditioner. Although this works wonderfully, it doesn't last long, maybe only about three or four days, but it is certainly better than nothing.

Sonrise Elementary School had a football field and a baseball diamond right there at the end of our street. All we had to do is cross the street and hop over a fence and we were there. Keith, Carrie, and a next door neighbor forced me to play baseball with them at the baseball diamond one day. I had trouble playing baseball because I was left-handed and everyone always made me bat or catch right-handed, so naturally I appeared uncoordinated. A car passed by and the next door neighbor flipped the driver off. Apparently he knew these people and had an altercation with them before involving his little sister. The three people in the car, while young, were still older and bigger than Keith, Carrie, or the neighbor and they started beating up Keith. Cars were driving by and telling the punk kids to leave Keith alone. Carrie had joined in to no avail and one of the older people got out and threatened the rest of us to stay put or else he would use a switchblade he had. But he was on the other side of the chain link fence. So when he taunted and insulted us, I taunted him back saying that he must be a very big person to have to threaten little kids with a knife. This pissed him off and the other kids yelled at me to stop, but I kept on talking. The punk started to climb the fence to come after us (me) and everyone panicked. I told everyone to take off in different directions so that it would be impossible for him to get all of us and whoever escaped could go get the police. I stayed behind and started shaking the fence so the punk kid couldn't climb it and kept slipping off. Some of the other kids joined me and the punk kid gave up.

Yet another time Keith and Carrie decided they wanted to play football with me at Sonrise, and I said no, that they were too big for me to play like that. They forced me to play and the next thing I knew, Keith tossed me the ball (I usually could not play catch because I was afraid of the ball when it was in motion) and told me to run. Carrie ran me down, stepped on my foot, and pushed me down. This caused excruciating pain in my foot and I had to literally crawl home and tell Trudy what happened. Trudy was afraid my foot had been broken and took me to the hospital. I was bedridden for an entire week after that until my foot recovered.

Once a week we were allowed to take a shower together in the Master Bathroom, as the other bathroom was reserved for the girls. One of those girls was five year old Alison, who was Fred and Trudy's real daughter. But this one time we went to take a shower, Alison was already in there, sitting naked on the toilet. As I looked at her, she stood up, flashed her butt, then her pudendum at us. Being five years old, she had no genital hair. The boys were unimpressed but I had never seen a naked girl before. So I got down on my hands and knees directly in front of her and told her to repeat that and she did. I was astonished. I mentioned out loud, "She looks the same, front to back, only different sizes".

While I was in Alabama visiting Trudy's mom, Keith and Carrie waited until I went to sleep one night and then pinned me down while a third kid (whose name I cannot remember) sodomized me. The kid had a little dick and I couldn't feel a thing. I never fell for those mind games about how I must have gotten raped because I was or made myself attractive to other men and therefore I must have been a latent homosexual.

A girl down the street came down to our house for a swim in our swimming pool. The Gestalt's had left and no adults were home. Keith and Carrie took advantage of the situation and the next thing I knew, Carrie got out of the pool and kept pushing the girl back into the water every time she tried to get out, while Keith would ride on top of her and hold her under water. When she came up for air, they would tell her to take her bikini off and flash her breasts at them. She refused until she could no longer take the punishment they were giving her. It was the first time I ever saw a grown woman's breast. I didn't understand what was happening next but I knew that whatever it was, it was very bad for her so I suddenly had an idea and as soon as I heard a car passing by, I said that I heard the Gestalt's pulling up in the driveway and into the garage. They weren't in the position to affirm or deny what I said and seeing as I extremely rarely ever lied, they took my word for it and let her go. Keith and Carrie got very upset when they saw that I was "mistaken" about the Gestalt's returning. She thanked me later for saving her life.

While I was at the Gestalt's, the social worker took me to see my biological mom. I think my mother was staying at a trailer park. She had a little girl staying with her (babysitting?), about the same age as me. She told us to go outside and play. We talked and the little girl asked me if I had ever had sex and had I ever kissed a girl. I felt uncomfortable because talking about sex was against the rules. So when we played hide and seek, I sneaked back to the trailer. My mom showed me a magazine she was collecting. It was a monthly magazine on anatomy and this issue was on women and was available at the newsstands. She flipped through some of the pages and showed me some very interesting things. I loved this magazine but I had no money, so once a month I went to Von's Supermarket just down the street and stole this magazine off the shelf.

At Royal Oak Intermediate School, a teacher there had a book that I fell in love with. It was an automotive mechanics book that her son had bought. For some reason other than my extreme interest in the book, the teacher bought me a copy of the book on Automotive Mechanics. She had signed it but I lost it over time, not realizing the sentimental value of a gift such as this until I was in my fifties. In hindsight, it amazes me that someone would do something like that for me for no reason other than to be kind but she was a woman and women can be so amazing sometimes.

Another book I loved to "read" was a dictionary. Trudy had a couple of dictionaries that were nice and thick and full of information.

I love to tell the truth, which is another very autistic trait. Autistic's hate lies and if left to their own devices, will avoid any and all lies. The problem is that the world thrives on lies; it is essential to be able to lie in society. If good ol' Aunt Agatha comes up to me and tells me that she is worried if her gorgeous new expensive red sweater makes her look a little fat or not, I will tell her the truth, no holds barred. If she is a very fat then she is very fat, regardless of whatever sweater she is wearing, and I will tell her so. If she didn't want to hear about how awfully fat she is, then why did she ask if she looked a little fat? Why would you want someone to lie to you or skirt around the truth or elaborate on the truth or tell a white lie when you asked for the truth? There are two things at work here: 1) As an Autistic I would rather be hurt by the truth than comforted by a lie, and 2) I think it is natural for Autistics and non-Autistics both, to practice the Golden Rule. Autistics want to hear the truth no holds barred whereas non-Autistics want to be let down in a gentle, roundabout way.

Yet sometimes lying is essential. For example, pretend you are a German citizen during Hitler's reign. You are harboring some Jews in order to protect them from persecution. Then the Gestapo comes knocking on your door and asks if you are harboring any Jews. What do you say? Do you tell the truth, betray the people you were supposed to be friends to, or do you lie by intentionally deceiving the Gestapo into believing you would never harbor any Jews? Even an Autistic would be hard pressed to justify telling the truth in this instance so we can use examples like this to show that sometimes lying can be good and even though we know that most of the time lying is bad.

I was obsessed with the charts and tables of almost any kind. One of my favorite pages to look at was the page on knots, all kinds of knots. It had maps of the world and listed all the elements of the Periodic Chart (as they knew them back then). A few really cool sections were at the back of the dictionary. There was a section on rhymes, a section on male names, female names, geographical gazetteer, the Greek alphabet, and so on. It never occurred to me that "normal" people didn't read dictionaries for pleasure. I was neglected and ignored and that allowed me to do whatever I felt like doing when I was "alone". While people picked on me and bullied me something awful because I was "strange", there were times when I could be as "strange" as I wanted to be. That was the only time I could really be happy.

There was another teacher at Royal Oak, Mrs. Johnson, who was also very nice to me. She was a black woman and I had a crush on her. She gave me a flute to use and play with and let me sneak into the library and read books at lunchtime. When Christmas time came around, she hung mistletoe in the doorway and I got caught with her under the mistletoe. We kissed (no not like that) and the class made fun of us, but I didn't care because I liked Mrs. Johnson so much. But our "affair" ended one day when I got in trouble for clowning around in class (something I ordinarily never did). I was a little too comfortable around her and thought I could get away with anything but I had never been in trouble before. So when Mrs. Johnson told me I had to stay after school for detention, I was extremely upset. I threw some chalk I had at her and ran out of the classroom and down to the boy's bathroom. Hiding out in the boy's bathroom was something I often did when I got upset but this was different since I was doing it during class. I was called into the Principal's Office and Mrs. Johnson never spoke to me again after that, which didn't matter since I went to a different school after that: Sonrise Elementary School.

One day Trudy asked if I had any friends and I told her no I didn't. Was there anybody I wanted to be friends with? No. Was there anybody at school that wanted to be friends with me? Not that I knew of. Did it bother me I didn't have any friends and nobody wanted to be friends with me? No. She said that wasn't good and she somehow arranged for me to "be friends" with a kid just down the street that I went to school with whose name was . . . Freddy. Somehow it seemed to me there were way too many "Freds" hanging around this foster home. So anyways, we started hanging out according to directions. One of my best memories with Freddy was playing with paper airplanes at Sonrise Elementary and having contests to see who could build a better paper airplane.

Because of the bullying I would often have temper tantrums and then runaway. I soon became an expert at running away but I was never serious about it. I would always return within half-an-hour. That is until one day I decided to take off and hide at the side of the house in a below ground cubby hole to the basement of my foster home. I curled up and lay there, deciding what I wanted to do next when I fell asleep. I woke up two hours later. People were out looking for me everywhere. I sneaked over to the front porch and stayed hidden by some bushes while I listened to Trudy and some woman talk about me. The woman dropped her car keys and looked over at me while she was bending down and said she found me. Trudy said she was very worried because they were at the time limit before they had to call the police as was required by law to do.

My previous strategy of having temper tantrums when being picked on by Keith and Carrie was no longer working—it was one of my many "mid-life crises" I had growing up. Keith and Carrie now resorted to kicking and torturing, but even this wasn't enough. They had started plotting how they were going to kill me. They had what I call "practice runs", trying to find some way to kill me and make it look like an accident. Because I ran away a lot, this made it easy for they could just say I ran away while I was out with them and they couldn't find me and . . . whatever.

The first attempt at my life was to abandon me in a very large drainage tunnel within walking distance to our house in West Covina. So they took me and walked with me a long ways down the tunnel until we came to a spot in the tunnel where there was a steeply sloping drop in the tunnel. We slipped and slid our way down this slope until we reached the bottom. Then they both took off back up the slope, helping each other along the way. I let them get away and then waited a short while. I then positioned myself over the expansion cracks that lined the floor of the tunnel, and used those to wedge my hands in to get back to the top, since the floor was otherwise too slippery to navigate. Of course, Keith and Carrie were very disappointed when they saw me walking towards them at the entrance to the tunnel.

So that attempt to ditch me for good failed and they tried another, and again it involved the tunnel. They took me down a side tunnel and showed me a ladder that went up something like 30 or 35 feet. At the top of this ladder was a small boxed in area—the receiving end of a street drain, the ones that lie at curb level. It was probably about three feet tall and five feet long. It had a manhole cover above it but it was way too heavy to even budge. Keith and Carrie left me there and told me not to go anywhere until they returned, otherwise they would kick my ass. They probably thought I was too afraid to crawl up or down the ladder anyways, because I was a weakling—which I was—but I didn't let them know I wasn't THAT afraid or THAT weak. Instead I let them think I was afraid but I also knew not to go back down once they left me because I knew they would be waiting for me if I did. So I waited until I thought that they would have for sure left me alone and then I listened. I could hear everything. I could hear cars and birds and the steady whine of the wind, but most importantly, I could hear the footsteps of pedestrians. I waited until a certain pair got close enough and then I stuck my hand out of the drain and then yelled. A man heard me and told me not to be afraid, then he called the police but it wasn't very long before Keith and Carrie came flying up the ladder and took me down and out the tunnel, only to have the police waiting for us at the entrance.

We vacationed in Utah in Fred's trailer on some isolated property up in the mountains. Bad things happened here too but the worst of it was when Keith and Carrie talked me into inadvertently hurting Alison. They told me that Alison was a thrill-seeker and that if I really liked her (which I did) and wanted her to like me back, that when we were on the seesaw on the property, I should make her go as high as I could and then let the seesaw suddenly drop. This sounded fun to me so I did it but it didn't turn out very well, because when Alison hit the ground, she broke her arm in two places. I told Alison what Keith and Carrie had told me and she did a wonderful thing that I will never forget, a thing only a woman would do—she forgave me, then and there, right on the spot. But Fred never ever talked to me again after that and from then on, whenever he looked at me, I could see hate in his eyes. There was no way I could explain that this wasn't my fault and I never intended any harm to Alison.

The opportunity for Keith and Carrie to kill me for good finally came one day. Fred decided to let Keith, Carrie, and me go down to his place of work for some summertime fun. His office building had a pool table and a snooker table and we played with those. We (I) explored the 18-wheelers in the back lot, but the real prize was the river park behind the back lot itself.

This river park was located by a freeway. The freeway itself was concrete and elevated about 30 feet above ground. As we drove along, I could see Fred's place of business on the right hand side of the freeway and the freeway was curved at this point so we made a semi-circle around it and then . . . we passed it by. We would get off on the next off-ramp and then we would go left instead of right. It would then look like we were getting back on the freeway but we would stay on the on-ramp and depart down the off-ramp since they were joined together as one. We would then make a right and a left and a right . . . it was confusing but fascinating at the same time. We would wind up on a road that dead-ended at Fred's place of business. We appeared to drive almost right out where we started out from. The drive alone to Fred's place was just the coolest experience to me.

The water flowed from left to right, looking at it from Fred's place of business. The freeway itself acted like covered parking for the river below and that is the place where all our adventures on this river started out from. The pool of water right by our lot had tiny little blue gill in it that Keith and Carrie could fish for. Keith and Carrie loved to fish. The river had weirs (low lying overflow dams) about five or six feet tall that retained mud and dirt and became the basis for reeds and various kind of water weeds to grow in. Ducks swam happily all throughout the area and were kept safe by the camouflaging of the reeds. In some places it was deep and in some places the water flowed very fast.

Shortly thereafter, Keith and Carrie had told us they had stolen a river raft from some Mexican kids and we went exploring with it. That is, until just a few days or weeks later, when those kids got their friends and stole it back. Then we were exploring by foot. A thirty minute walk upstream was a large dam. It had three very large holes in it, about five or six feet tall, and they shot out water for a huge distance.

One day Keith and Carrie asked me and Richard to follow them. They said there was something that "we had to see". As we arrived at our destination, the first thing I saw was a heavy machinery hoe that had dredged a small channel alongside the river bank. I immediately sensed that something wrong because there were no workers present and I could see up and down the river bank for at least one mile in each direction. Then Keith and Carrie told me that the hoe wasn't what they wanted to show me. The small channel ended at an entrance way to a culvert. This entrance to this culvert had a widely-spaced wire grate over it and it passed through the concrete river bank over to what appeared to be a park or something similar. Tremendous amounts of water were shooting out of it for hundreds of feet on the other side of the outlet. Normally this culvert was covered over by very thick steel plating that was cut into strips and welded into a weave pattern but it was left off while the workers were away. This was very disturbing to me because I knew that heavy machinery wasn't supposed to be unattended and if the workers had left, surely they would have followed common sense safety protocols and at least covered up the culvert so no one could accidentally stumble into it. Keith and Carrie directed me and Richard to stand by the western edge of the drain. The entryway to the culvert was probably about eight feet long and was filled with water four or five feet deep, with the water was being drawn into it at such a rate that little whirlpools appeared on the surface and made little sucking noises. The drain itself was about three or four feet in diameter. Again we were directed to wait while Keith and Carrie disappeared behind us and out of nowhere a duck appeared. We were told to watch. The duck quacked in fear; I could feel the fear in its voice but it wouldn't fly away. I didn't understand why it wouldn't fly away but in hindsight I guess they must have captured it earlier and broken its wings. The duck suddenly dove under the water and spiraled around like a football and disappeared from sight. While we watched this, Carrie had joined us at the northern edge of the drain whereas Keith had sneaked up behind me (I could see his shadow). I turned around and saw a strange look in his eyes and I knew whatever he was thinking, it wasn't good, so I grabbed the lapels of Keith's shirt as hard as I could because I knew it would be hard to get me off easily (I had done this before so I know that this technique would work to stall for time) and then I swung myself out over the drain, putting all my weight into it. Keith was terrified and I screamed over and over, "I don't want to die! I don't want to die!". Keith asked what I wanted him to do and that I was hurting his back. I told Richard and Carrie to move away from us and then I told Keith to back up and keep backing up until we were about 15 feet away from the edge of the drain. I let go and Keith joined Carrie at the northern edge of the drain. I had dodged the bullet, so to speak. That's when I noticed an 8-year old boy holding hands with a 5-year old girl about 300 feet away and they were walking towards us. Apparently, Keith and Carrie noticed them too and they ran over to them. The heavy machinery hoe was in the way of whatever was happening so I couldn't see what Keith and Carrie were doing, but I knew there was a struggle and the end result was I saw the little boy suddenly appear at the entrance way to the culvert, which placed him about eight feet from the drain itself. As

> Although I had seen Carrie drown the little girl and do a little dance with the corpse afterwards, I had no feelings for the demise of the girl because in my mind I didn't know her. People believe that means that autistic people are without empathy, but that isn't true. I would never murder a little girl because I have an unrepressed empathy for the pain and suffering I can cause others by my actions but watching the little girl die was not something directed at me. Once she was dead, there was nothing left to feel for her anyways because she was "gone". Richard was still scared to death even after our way home after the murders, but I did not feel fear because in my mind the danger had already passed. I recognized that I had been through a dangerous situation with very bad people but the opportunity for harm had passed. I am not so much interested what has passed as I am in what is present. The future, on the other hand, is only important to me when I can predict its outcome.

he approached the mouth of the entrance way, he cried out, "I can feel it from here", which I presume to mean he could feel the suction of the drain. He disappeared back where he came from for a few seconds and then reappeared again, and he waded along the edge of the drain and then looked up at me and Richard then said, "Tell someone what happened here". Incredibly, the boy waded up right next to the drain by shimmying along the concrete sides of the culvert without getting sucked in. Keith came over and told us it was time for us to go and we started to walk together and go back to Fred's trucking business and that's when I saw Carrie in the water, holding the little girl underwater. Her hands were outstretched in front of her, and her hands were formed in the shape that you see when you are going to scratch someone's eyes out in a fight. Carrie yelled to Keith for us to go back and we did, but only for one or two minutes, and then we resumed our march back to Fred's workplace again. As we passed by Carrie, this time the little girl, who was obviously dead, was propped up against Carrie's chest with one hand around her waist and his right hand was outstretched and holding her left hand as if he was dancing with her and he was singing, trying very hard to pretend that she was still alive and they were just having fun. As Richard and I continued marching to Fred's workplace, I looked back and saw Carrie get out of the water by himself and join Keith at the bottom end of the culvert. They were throwing rocks at something (presumably the boy) in the drain. As I watched them, they were suddenly startled by something they saw (presumably the little girl's body had floated downstream into the drain by then), and stopped throwing rocks. A heard a strange brief sound but it wasn't a sucking noise like you would expect, but it sounded like a chipper. I saw water splash up on the concrete bank surrounding the culvert entrance way. Keith and Carrie then excitedly ran over and caught up with us.

As we were driving home that day and we rounded along the on-ramp to the freeway, Fred suddenly stopped the truck we were in and we all turned around to look. What we saw was incredible. There were so many cop cars, I couldn't count them all, and they all had their emergency lights on. There were so many emergency lights on that all I could see was bunch of blue lights and instead of being able to see individual lights of each cop car, all I could see was a weird scintillation of lights. I learned that water as powerful as I had seen would have been powerful enough to shred bodies or at least mangle them so that almost every bone in their body would have been broken. Thankfully Keith and Carrie didn't force us to watch the bodies as they got mangled.

A policeman/detective came over to Fred's place of work the next day and conducted interviews with Keith, Carrie, Richard, and me. Keith and Carrie threatened harm to me and Richard if we said anything but I would have told the cop everything if only the cop hadn't of been so stupid. Keith and Carrie had a habit of listening in on conversations in the room that the cop was in. They would hide around the corner and nobody would notice they were there. I know this because they had listened in on a conversation that Fred and I had one day when I got in trouble for something and Fred wanted to lecture me for. As the cop talked, I kept looking back out the doorway. I think he was mystified by my actions but didn't say anything. He asked if I knew anything about some kids drowning, and I shook my head yes. I asked what protection but he wouldn't say, so I didn't trust him and said nothing. If this cop had a social worker with him, waiting to whisk me away immediately, I would have told him everything. Then I vaguely remember him saying something about four people drowning, and not two, so I thought he must be talking about a different murder. It wasn't until years later that I put two-and-two together and realized that if Keith and Carrie had killed the two workers present at that worksite at that time, it would explain why the workers weren't anywhere around to be seen when I was there. It would explain why Keith and Carrie had no fear of getting caught (I was expecting the workers to return at any second but they never did) and why Keith and Carrie had enough time to capture a duck and keep it tied up or whatever they did with it until they could take the time to go back to Fred's trucking business and get me and Richard. I vaguely remember Keith and Carrie later on telling me how they had killed the workers and that they went to look at the bodies and they were like "rubber dolls". The detective I mentioned here also called my new foster parents at a different foster home I had moved into and asked them to ask me if I had anything I wanted to say to him. I initially said yes but then the foster parents told me I would have to tell them everything first and then they would give that information to the cop. I said no way, I had nothing to say. I didn't trust my new foster parents at all but you can read all about that in the next chapter. Just think about it—if that cop had only come down to the foster home, took me to McDonald's and bought me a Happy Meal, I would have told him everything. Either the cops know nothing about child psychology, or I didn't act like a non-autistic child would have acted under the same circumstances.

I failed to mention something that happened quite some time before all this occurred. Something I thought best saved for after the preceding story instead of before it, something that puts Keith in a different light than you have seen him so far. You see, Keith had some rabbits that he loved and took care of. In the back yard, a small area was wire-chained fenced off and in that area were the cages for the rabbits. Keith bred the rabbits but he had an issue: Whenever Trudy's old pet poodle would find a way to get in the fenced off area, the poodle would immediately head for the rabbit cages—which were suspended off the ground—at just the right height so a fat, short poodle could walk under it and bite the legs off the baby rabbits. Sometimes the babies would live, but most of the time they would not. Whenever there was a baby that looked like it wasn't going to make it, Keith, if I remember correctly, was

> Professor Snape was portrayed as an evil person all throughout the Harry Potter series until the very end where we see that deep down inside, Snape was a good person. Sometimes it is hard to see the good that exists in evil people but it is there, somewhere, hidden, but still alive. All it takes to revive it is a little regret and the love of a woman. Snape loved and respected Lillian (Harry Potter's mother) and Snape projected that love and respect onto Harry himself because Harry was a part of Lillian. Snape wanted to be evil but his regret at having lost Lillian kept him from fully submitting himself to evil.

forced by Trudy to drown the babies. By hand. By himself. Keith hated that poodle with a passion but could do nothing to it without getting into serious trouble (mainly without terminating their agreement they had to get his brother, Carrie, and bring him into their family). Keith tried to hold back the tears, and it made his eyes watery and red, but his expression and behavior was something new I didn't understand at that time. All I knew was what a horrible mind altering effect killing the baby rabbits was having on his personality. Keith was very angry afterward, slamming the gate closed and things like that. I tried to avoid him the rest of the day. Keith gave up on raising rabbits because of that poodle and its owner, but I know in my heart that Keith never gave up on the thought of having to kill those rabbits. Trudy should have been there for Keith but Trudy was one of those rare women, the kind of women that have lost their healing touch. Be thankful there are not many women out there like that. I'm not saying Keith wasn't an "evil" person or that he had an excuse for everything he did, I am just trying to make you understand that it is easy to be quick and judge people but often times there is more than meets the eye.

Of course, the story doesn't end there either. Keith did wind up killing the poodle. I don't know how, but what I do remember is that Keith asked me to sit down on an upside-down planter next to the pool one day and just wait there for a second. It was early morning and something was not right: I was sitting on a planter in the middle of some landscaping for no reason. Next thing I knew, Keith and Trudy came outside and said they were looking for the poodle. Trudy asked why I was sitting all alone on a planter in the middle of all those white landscaping rocks. I got up and Keith overturned the planter and the poodle was there, dead. Trudy was very upset and I told her the truth about what happened, but she acted like she didn't know what to believe.

The Hippos'

SOMETIME IN 1971: CAROLYN and William J Hippos in Temple City. I was 11 years old.

The social worker had told me that I was going to live with this man, a man whom you could say that we "had a lot in common". He allegedly was a "gentle man" and they thought he would be good for me. Well this man was gentle, in public, but in private it was a different matter. As for what we had in common, my new foster father was "intellectually challenged". He was what in psychology would be called a "high functioning adult"—"high functioning" only meaning that he had an IQ above 70. Just the thought that the foster care system equated me with mental retardation was humiliating.

Bill and his entire family had buck teeth and loud whiney, horsey sounding laughs and sometimes I felt embarrassed being seen with him in public. My peers would privately make fun of Bill as a mental retard, whenever they saw him, and I didn't relish the thought that these same kids would start calling me retarded by association, although they never did. In fact, it was just the opposite. The teachers would always tell me how smart I was and that I was a "little professor" which, when they said it in front of Bill, and I could tell by the look in his eyes that this only made him feel stupid, which in turn made him resent me. Our relationship wasn't as good of a match as the foster care system blindly assumed it would be.

I can empathize with Bill's reaction when people told him how smart I was. Many parents of autistic children like to say that Einstein, Mozart, Newton, or Bill Gates were autistic. The problem with being compared to people like that, is that the vast majority of Autistics will not make it to that status, therefore the vast majority of Autistics are being shown what failures they are because they won't make it. If the people in that list were actually autistic, it does us no good to know this unless they can tell us how they survived or overcame autism, but we never have that information.

It is ignorant to compare us to people that are only merely autistic-like. "Autistic-like" only means they are not autistic, that they have some but not all of the qualities required to be diagnosed as autistic, singular qualities which you could almost apply to anyone in the world, and therefore has no meaning. I think the real reason for saying that people like Einstein, Mozart, Newton, or Bill Gates were "potentially autistic" is to pacify the adults of autistic children. It is meant to make the adults feel better at the expense of making the children feel worse.

It is even more ridiculous to compare us to people that don't exist in real life, "people" like Rainman or Forest Gump or MOZART AND THE WHALE or Napoleon Dynamite.

I suppose all of that is still better than being called creepy, goofy, weird, quirky, loser, jerk, demon possessed, and retarded—all things that I have been called, but I would much rather not be compared to anybody, real or imagined, I just want to be accepted for who I am so I can just be myself, without judgment.

I had a strange habit, namely, I cussed all the time. Something compelled me to cuss at anyone or anything, including Carol. I never understood why people cussed and then turn around and say how cussing is such a bad thing to do. They would cuss so casually amongst themselves all the time that it seemed natural to talk that way. People thought it was funny to listen to comedians cuss on TV. What I didn't understand and still don't understand all too well even today is, not that cussing is wrong, but it is only sometimes wrong, under certain arbitrary circumstances. What those circumstances were, I could never figure out because it is one of the many "unwritten rules" of socializing that have made no logic or sense.

Cussing is so illogical. Take for example, the word "fuck". It has no real meaning. It can be a very good word or a very bad word, or it can be an adjective or a verb, all depending on context and your imagination. I can say you are fucking great or I can say you are a fucking idiot or I can say let's fuck and the word has a totally different meaning in each case. You can even fucking use the word fuck anywhere in a fucking sentence and it will still make fucking sense. How can that be? Fuck violates all the rules of linguistics. You could replace the word "fuck" with any other 4- or 5-letter nonsensical word and it wouldn't change a thing, say for example, the word "Smurf". I can still say "Smurfing" is just one of those Smurfing words that fit any Smurfing where in a Smurfing sentence and it still Smurfing makes sense. I can also say you are Smurf-tastic or Smurf-alicious or I can say you're a Smurfing idiot. And Smurf has the added benefit of being a proper noun, so I could even say you are a son-of-a-Smurf. You can't do that with the word "fuck".

Anyway, one day I cussing at/with Carol—I have no idea what the conversation was about—but I do know that Bill used this as an excuse to whip me. I had welt marks all over my body. I wish I would have realized then just how terrible what Bill had done to me and reported him to my social worker.

A spanking can be punishment or it can be torture—it all depends on how angry you are when dealing out the spanking and how much self-control you have. Most men don't have that much self-control when it comes to managing their anger. Bill would spank me as hard as he could until it left welts. To make matters worse, I was 15 years old and yet he still spanked me as if I were a 5 year old. There is nothing any child could ever do that would justify abuse or torture. If you, as an adult, cannot reason with a child and feel you have to resort to violence, intimidation, or humiliation to force them to submit to your will, you are not fit to be a parent.

I remember this crush I had on this girl, Pamela. On my way to school every day, I would stop by a certain house and get little flowers from it, then pull petals off of each flower, one at a time, saying "She loves me, she loves me not" until I found one that ended in "She loves me". Of course, she really never did love me.

Date unknown: 16997 Main St in La Puente. In the back of our house was an old abandoned dump yard. One day me and my foster brother were riding our bikes around in the dump yard and we came across some kids (two boys and a girl) playing on a raft in a small pond that had formed in the middle of the dump yard. The water was a very murky and dark green. As I watched, I saw the little girl quietly slip off the raft into water. They couldn't find her in the water and one of the boys had to run home and call 911. The remaining boy asked me to help him find his sister and I said no way. The last thing I wanted to do was grope in the dark for a dead body. We stayed until the firetruck appeared and then we left.

I watched my next door neighbor get into a fight one day. I didn't understand what they were doing or why anyone would fight. As I watched, the bigger guy who was allegedly winning, fell on his knee and broke his leg. As he was writhing in pain, his older brother came out and chased the other guy away.

My foster brother hated Carol so one day he got a black widow from the backyard (there were always lots of black widows in the backyard) and he took it inside the house and put it beneath the covers on Carol's side of the bed. The next morning I was awakened by the sound of Carol crying and moaning in the bathroom. Next thing I knew she was rushed off to the hospital and we had the day off from school.

In order to try to prevent me from wetting my bed, the Hippos' would not let me drink anything after I got home from school. On vacation they wouldn't let me drink all day long. We were up at Lake Isabella, a place which was hot and dry that time of the year we were there and I was dehydrated. I was also severely sunburned because they said I was too white and needed some color, so they made me stay out in the sun all day without a shirt on. I had no idea what child abuse was, which was too bad, because if I had of known, I would have left the Hippos' then and there and saved myself a lot of grief. Anyway, the other couple they had gone on the trip with had offered me a tall glass of some Kool-Aid and I swigged it down with one gulp. Then they offered me another and another. The Hippos' complained but the couple didn't pay any heed to them. I literally drank a gallon of Koolaid right then and there. The next morning I got very sick from being sunburned. The day after that we returned home but the couple called up and (correctly) accused the Hippos' of child abuse but it was of no use. Bill told them he wanted nothing to do with them ever again and hung up the phone.

I had two personal bullies of my own at Giano Intermediate School. They were high school jocks that, like the stereotypical jock, were muscular and popular and had lots of girlfriends. What they would do is wait for me to get out of P.E. (Physical Education). I would roll my gym clothes up in a real tight little cylinder—perfect for them to throw like a football in front of the whole school. The "football" never held together for very long when it would "explode" and rain down onto some tumbleweeds and I would have to go over and retrieve my jock strap, shorts, and t-shirt in front of all the (mostly) pretty Pachuca (gangsta girls) and caliente chicas (cute chicks). Then one day the principal came over and caught them doing this to me. He had them go over and pick up my jock strap, shorts, and t-shirt and return it to me in a nice, neat little tight cylinder. Then I never saw them again.

Some of the girls at Giano were nice enough to not ever tease me about this public bullying but not the Pachucas. Being autistic, I only had an extremely small chance of ever having a girlfriend under normal circumstances but with the bullying and prejudice, it was impossible. For example, a group of Pachucas came over to me and another white kid at lunch one day. This kid was tall and blond and I guess you could say he was a "pretty boy". I guess you could also say that he was racist because these Pachucas came over and started harassing the both of us, knocking our lunches and school books over onto the ground. They kept asking the kid if he liked Hispanic girls and if not, why not. We would both pick up our school books and they would knock them back onto the ground again. But the Pachucas left me alone after they asked me if I liked Hispanic girls or not, after one of them sat down beside me and I said yes, I did like some Hispanic girls, including the pretty one sitting next to me.

Yet another time some Pachucos came over at lunchtime and beat up another white kid I was hanging out with. The kid asked why I didn't help him out and I said I had no beef with the Pachucos and the Pachucos had no beef with me so obviously he did or said something to piss them off and I wasn't going to start something for no good reason. He walked away and as he was walking away, he said we could never, ever be friends. I thought that well, he started trouble on his own so why was I supposed to help him make enemies for no good reason other than he was stupid? That's nonsense!

Lunchtime was obviously a dangerous time to be in, so I think you could understand why at lunchtime, I had a very rigid routine that consisted of walking the campus and picking up the spare change that people would discard on the ground. It was apparently some kind of Mexican custom to leave a little spare change on the ground. I would acquire enough change to buy a chocolate shake almost every day doing this. Afterwards, I would go into the library and spend the rest of my lunch time there reading every science/technical/UFO book I could find. I loved it.

As I was getting in my locker one day to put away one set of books and get out another set, a big kid—another jock—came into the locker area. Now the locker area was not a very big area and it was caged in so there was only one way in or out of the area. He let everyone else leave but blocked my way until I was the only one left. I told him I had to get to class and to let me pass but he said no. He knocked my books out of my hands and I picked them up. He then knocked my books out of my hands and I picked them up again. He kept doing this and I told him he couldn't keep doing this forever so what was his point? He said he didn't have to keep up, all he had to do was wear me down. Wear me down and do what? He said he wanted me to suck his dick and I told him there was no way I was going to do that. I was never going to get tired of picking up my books over and over again. He pulled down his zipper and repeated his previous statement. Fortunately another jock came in and pushed the punk out of my way and told me to go. I started to pick up my books and he said forget my books, just run. So I ran out and told the teachers what happened. I did learn something valuable from this experience because later on I would be put in an orphanage and I was able to recognize the kind of situations and people that would try and "punk" other kids, and thereby it taught me how to stay out of trouble.

In the P.E. locker room showers one day, one of the bullies went berserk. He enjoyed dipping one end of a gym towel in water and snapping it at me. I knew what to do and how to avoid being zapped and this frustrated him so much that he started snapping the towel at lots of other kids. I called for the coach and the coach came out and when this bully zapped the coach, they started fighting. I ran out of the locker room but the next day the bully was gone and the coach returned. It was horrible because the iris of one eye of the coach was red. He rounded up the bullied kids and told them not to worry about anything anymore, that the bully had been taken care of by the proper authorities.

A substitute teacher had taken over a class of mine one day. She was an older woman—and very racist. Two Pachucas were picking on me, calling me names, and the substitute teacher asked why I put up with that crap from "those dirty little spic bitches". I was terrified. I wasn't racist and I didn't want anyone to think that I was. Sure these two Pachucas were bad people, but there were some very nice Mexican girls in my class and I told the substitute teacher this. I told her you couldn't judge an entire race by two assholes (you should have seen the looks on the Pachuca's faces when I said that) when there were these lovely, intelligent girls like the one I was sitting next to. Why can't you judge an entire race by girls like that? I told her that in respect for all the nice girls in the world, like the one sitting next to me, I wasn't going to stay there and listen to her hate-filled crap and I walked out. It was something I never did before—talk back to a teacher—especially since I loved school so much. I didn't want to be a trouble maker but this was what trouble makers did. Then to my surprise, the whole entire class followed me out the door and no one ever picked on me in that school ever again.

Date unknown: The Hippos' had relocated to 442 E Haltern, Glendora. The Hippos' hated me and my bed wetting so they went so far as to force me to hang my stained sheets up outside and take them down in the evening, every single day. They made it very clear this was to embarrass me to quit wetting my bed. Even if I had any friends, I couldn't invite them to my house because of the shame, not to mention the smell of urine in my bedroom. Conversely, I couldn't have any sleepovers because of the high potential for extreme embarrassment.

There were two kids that came to live with the Hippos': Jackie and Jay. Jackie was five years old and Jay was four. One day I saw both of them in their room and they were lying on their beds and arching their backs. Jackie was giving instructions on how to masturbate. Of course these instructions were all wrong for a boy to follow but I watched Jackie (who was doing it wrong even for a girl) and then asked her what she thought she was doing. She said it was supposed to feel good and her babysitter had taught her this. I told her that if any of her foster parents saw her doing this, she would be in deep trouble, so I asked her not to do that.

One night, she and I were staying up late all alone and unsupervised. We were watching Godzilla. We were together under one blanket by the TV, as this is how Caroline had arranged things before she went to bed and left us all alone. As Jackie and I watched TV, we snuggled together. I was thinking to myself that I would never ever have a girlfriend because I was a "loser" and I wet my bed anyway, and Jackie had always been nice to me, and I thought Jackie would be the closest thing I could ever have as a girlfriend. So I asked her if she wanted me to "rub her bellybutton" but I didn't rub her bellybutton and instead I masturbated her to orgasm. I enjoyed making her feel good and she loved it so much she was constantly asking me to "rub her bellybutton" after that. I did that a few more times but then told her it that it was wrong of me to do that to her and she shouldn't ask me to do that anymore.

Carol decided to take me along with her on a long drive outside of the Los Angeles metropolitan area. Along a long, deserted stretch of highway was a motel. There was nothing else for miles and miles around. Carol had me wait in the Volkswagen dune buggy while she went in and "talked". This was so weird. She came back outside and we took off again. We drove along for a long time and found another isolated motel. We repeated the same scenario. Carol was upset and drove back to the first motel. She went inside and was obviously angry but she came back out and we went home. I never felt comfortable about whatever Carol was up to that day. It is only in hindsight, many many years later, that I finally understood what Carol was up to. I talked to one of my co-workers at a company I worked for years later and she said she thought Carol wanted to rape me that day—which in hindsight makes sense. Carol and William couldn't have children of their own up until then and that might have had something to do with this incident. I don't know. I am just thankful that even criminals, like the ones who rent out cheap, sleazy motels on an hourly basis, even they had limits as to what they morally would or would not do.

I went to Carl Sandberg JR High School in Glendora, California when I turned 13. There was this bully who hung out at the bike rack. His main target was me, although he would occasionally pick on other kids. What he would do is wait for me to be distracted, mainly when I had to reach over mine and other people's bikes adjacent to mine, and lock my bike to the rack. This bully would time his takeoffs so that he could collide with me at just the right speed and instant of time to see if I would "fly". Well one day his wish came true. I had successfully avoided him until then, no thanks to the adults who never paid any attention to my pleas for help. He struck me and I literally flew through the air a few feet and landed on my toes. No damage done but it could have been serious. Fortunately a concerned adult in the administration office—that just so happens to overlook the bike rack—saw this and immediately came out and took the both of us to the Principal's Office. I didn't stay long before they asked me to leave, but not before I overheard something about ". . . to Juvenile Hall again". The bully started ranting and raving, only by me interrupting him and telling him that wasn't this exactly what you wanted to happen by doing what you did? But that only made him yell and scream all the louder, so I left and went home.

Up until the Ninth Grade, I was way behind everyone else in my run times or my ability to compete in sports. How could I when I was 4'10" and 60 pounds? I had stagnated at this height and weight ever since I was probably about nine years old. One day I was getting dressed after a P.E. session at my school. As always, I never showered with the other kids; I just went straight to my locker and exchanged my

Without a source of emotion, especially affection, somewhere in your life, you WILL die, not immediately but with time your body will start shutting down. I should know, that's what failure-to-thrive and deprivation dwarfism is all about: extreme emotional neglect. I often see lots of woman where I can see and feel their love. I don't ever see very many loving men. Why is that? Is it because women are preprogrammed to give birth to life and then nurture it? Men can only protect life or take life, not make it worth living. I see this demonstrated even when it comes to autism, for example, I see WOMEN FOR AUTISM on Twitter but never a corresponding MEN FOR AUTISM. When I go to autism conventions, I've seen far more women than men there. Even local meetups are filled with lots of women and very few men, for example, I have seen MOTHERS OF CHILDREN WITH AUTSIM but never a corresponding FATHERS OF CHILDREN WITH AUTISM.

People have great trust in technology. There is absolutely nothing wrong with technology. Great things have been accomplished by technology. Yet the world is not sustained or dependent on technology, it is sustained and dependent on economics. When our current economy disintegrates and fails, so will everything else that depends on it, including technology. Without money, there can be no technology. That includes medical and manufacturing. The world will be broken and unless women true to their nature are there to put it back together again, humans will go extinct due to extreme emotional neglect.

workout clothes for my street clothes. But while I was getting dressed, another kid was watching me. I asked why he was watching me and he told me it was because I had no genital hair. I thought, "So what?", but then he decided to tell the P.E. coach. The coach came out and examined me and said this isn't right. He told me to immediately seek medical attention. I guess this issue was more important than I thought so I mentioned it to my foster parents, who could have cared less. The next day my P.E. coach asked me what happened to his request and I told him that my foster parents could care less. The P.E. coach called my social worker and they forced my foster parents to get me treated. At first the doctor talked about giving me growth hormone shots from cadavers, but then later on he said they discovered a new treatment using testosterone. I went from 4'10"60# to 5'7"100# in nine months flat. The real question was, why? Why did I fail to physically stay up with the rest of my peers from 5th grade to 9th grade? The answer didn't lie in me; it lied within the foster care system. I was in a world that didn't want me, need me, or love me, and this was having an effect on me physically.

If a child is physically and emotionally neglected to an extreme—and by physical, I mean by touching and caressing and holding a child—one of two things will happen: 1) That child will fail to thrive and they will die, or 2) That child will fail to thrive and acquire deprivation dwarfism. The dividing line between these two things is age. If the child being neglected is two years or younger, they will die. If the child being neglected is two years or older, they will acquire deprivation dwarfism. I was the latter. My failure to thrive has detrimentally affected me physically in many ways, for example, all but my front teeth are half the height they should be so my teeth don't come together unless I move my lower jaw back while I chew. This is because my adult teeth came in while I was still 4'10" and are proportional for that size instead of the 5'11" that I am today. I learned the value of emotions through my deprivation dwarfism. Depravation dwarfism is a derivative of the failure to thrive, and the failure to thrive is the result of extreme emotional neglect. This demonstrates that without emotions, you will die, that's how important emotions are. What is so interesting was that I was so extremely neglected and not a single person ever took notice, except for my 9th grade coach.

In eighth grade I fell in love with this girl in my chemistry class, Susan Montmarquet. It was one of these "admire her from a distance" kinds of things. Then I got this paper route and wouldn't you know it, my route took me right past her house. I always had extra papers left over for some reason, so I decided that I would do something nice for her father and leave a free paper on his doorstep every day. I thought if I could make her father happy, it would make Susan happy as well. Apparently this worked and I won over Susan's heart. I know this because one day I went over to her house to see what happened to her because I hadn't seen her at school for over a week. Well she was sick and in bed and her father invited me in to see her. I was happy but terrified at the same time. I knew I couldn't consummate our relationship the way lovers should because I knew I could never spend the night with her (since I wet my bed), I had no car, and I didn't know where I was going to be living next because I knew that I couldn't stay at the abusive home I was at. Not long after that, a drunk driver hit me on my bike and without a bike I could no longer have a paper route.

It was a nice, cold winter in Los Angeles (LA) and it was a clear Saturday morning so my foster parents got the urge to play in the snow—as did everybody else in LA it seemed. We took a two hour trip up to Big Bear and the place was packed! Then they saw a snowmobile rental with some guys out front waving motorists down and offering them to play in the snow in their lot—for a small fee. There was a small hill at the back of the lot that was "perfect" for sliding down on inner tubes. What concerned me was the snowmobile parts lined up alongside a fence—the side closest to where Bill told me to place my inner tube— and inner tubes were not designed to be steerable in snow. I told him no, it was too dangerous, but he threatened to throw me down the hill if I didn't comply. So the next thing I knew, I suddenly veered toward the lot fence at a high speed, with my little four-year old foster brother, Jay, hitching a ride on my back. If I flipped the inner tube now, my little foster brother would suffer, so I hoped for the best and experienced the worst. I hit a fence pole probably doing about 20 or 25 miles an hour. Luckily I missed

The scar on my forehead is the corresponding version of the lightning scar that Harry Potter has on his forehead.

all the very dangerous snowmobile parts lying around. After the collision, the inner tube and I shot out back into the middle of the lot and I flipped the inner tube there, and then the blood just started gushing out, as head wounds typically do. My scar cost me 27 stitches on my forehead. The embarrassment of having to go to school on Monday, with my stitches hanging out for the entire world to see made me feel like a freaking Frankenstein.

I was enrolled in Wrestling. I was in the Feather Weight division due to my low weight (5'7"100#). I had no one who was in my division at school so the coach had me practice wrestle a much larger person as there was only one other wrestler available at this time. The coach would then leave us all alone. While the coach was gone, this much larger person would try to pick me up off the ground, hold me as high as he could over his head, and slam me to the ground. Most of the time he would fail because I could subvert his attempts in many ways. Sometimes I would pretend to be very compliant and right when he was ready to slam me, I would grab onto his arm or his neck on the way down. These were the only times I was able to hurt him. One time he successfully slammed me to the ground and then I played dead. It made him happy and even more determined to hurt me. Finally the coach came in one day and saw what was happening and that ended that.

In tenth grade, I met this girl while I was in Track and Field. I was forced by the Hippos' to participate in sports events, so I chose the 100 yard dash. During summer school this beautiful Mexican-looking girl would talk to me and she would ask me over to her house for lunch. She was so nice. After practice one day, we both were walking together across the field behind the gym and there were these two boys—punks—and for sport they were throwing a discus at people walking by. I told this girl to wait and I timed our approach so as to avoid these deadly implements. We stopped to talk for a while by the parking lot by the west side of the gym when we heard sirens and saw a fire truck and ambulance pass us by and go into the field we had just traversed. It didn't take long before we found out that a girl had been struck by a discus and severely injured. We told the firemen that we had seen the two boys throwing the discus at passer-byes. We never saw either the girl or the two boys ever again after that.

But I did see this sexy girl again. I went to her house at the bottom of Glendora Mountain at lunchtime. One day she took me to her bedroom and lay on the floor, telling me not to think or say dirty thoughts as she spread her legs and made some sexually provocative poses and noises. It drove me crazy so I told her I was leaving . . . now! She got upset and she called out to her sister for help and she and her older sister asked what was wrong and I told her, I was asked not to think dirty thoughts and all I could do was think dirty thoughts. Her older sister asked what kind of thoughts would that be and I told her I wanted to make her sister scream by giving her cunnilingus. She asked why would I want to do that and I said because I heard it was the most pleasurable thing a woman could have done for her. So I left. Later on the sexy girl and I talked again and she said she was sorry and if I wanted to, her older sister would let me perform cunnilingus on her, but I said no. It was her that I wanted to make feel good and I didn't know her older sister enough to want to make her feel good. So I never saw those girls again after that.

One day while playing in the front yard, I said something which the Hippos' didn't like, so they asked me why didn't I run out into the street and "get masticated by a car". Their use of words was incorrect but I feel that they meant something very hateful by it. It was a very scary feeling.

Talk about scary; what happened next was the last straw, even for an autistic person like me. The Hippos' asked me if I wanted to go to the beach to have some fun swimming. It was a hot summer day and it sounded nice but their intentions were anything but nice. They took me to a beach and there were lots of people everywhere and crowds were an aversive to me and they knew it. They would then ask me if I wanted to go swimming here or there, and I would say no. So they kept on walking and asking until we came upon an area with large warning signs and no people in it. They ignored the huge, plainly visible warning signs even after I pointed it out to them. Bill said this was it, now was my chance to go for a swim. I looked at the water and how it bobbed up and down and it looked very dangerous. There was no sandy beach, only a small rocky ledge and I could tell that we were standing on the top of an otherwise underwater rocky cliff with the water just kissing the very top corner of the cliff. There was almost no surf and ocean waves would come in and just bounce off of the cliff and reflect back into the ocean. I said no, I wasn't going swimming in that and Bill told me to either jump in or he would throw me in. I thought about it and decided it would be better if I jumped in on my own because at least then I could time the waves and have a chance of jumping in at a safe(r) time. So I waited and then jumped and swam as far from the shore as I could. I didn't want to take a chance of being smashed against the cliff by the waves. But something else more dreadful happened. There were rip currents here but instead of taking you out to sea, they would drag you down to the bottom of the underwater cliff. I felt the water changing directions, took a few breaths, and let it suck me down. It forced me down all the way to the bottom of the underwater cliff. I was so deep underwater that it was dark. The bottom layer of mud looked white on the surface but that was just a light coating of something else on a black and very sticky mud. The current would force me down into that mud, clear up to my ankles. I thought I might never escape so I wiggled my feet as I waited for the current to change direction, so as to not be trapped when it did. I had a plan and the plan was to move diagonally with the current every time it changed direction and either pinned me down in the mud or shot me to the surface. I bobbed with the rip current this way a couple of times until I got right next to the breakwater. Then I had to time my landing so I would land on top of these very large hexagonal shaped concreted blocks, again so I wouldn't get smashed against them by the waves. So I finally escaped. Apparently, I had made this look easy and Carol and Bill asked me how the water was and thinking they had the nerve to ask me if I had enjoyed such a terrifying experience, I lied and said it was fun. Bill, being the "macho man" that he was, apparently didn't want to be outdone by a wimpy little kid like me, took off his shirt and jumped in, only he was having a terrible time trying to stay alive. Carol asked me to jump back in and save Bill but I just stood there and said and did nothing. Luckily two lifeguards came by and told us to back away. They threw Bill a lifesaver, which he eventually caught and was pulled safely ashore. These men seemed impressed by me. They asked how I survived and I said I didn't know and they said they had known divers who had been drowned in these waters so it was a miracle that I survived.

I had had enough mistreatment from the Hippos' so I stole Carol's personal phone book and found the number to the social worker. I called the social worker and left a few messages but nothing ever happened. I received no visit and no one ever talked to the Hippos'. Then one night after being yelled at for some insignificant reason, I ran away. I told one of my classmates, Scott's mom, about it, since we often hung out together, not because we were friends but because (as I found out a year or two later) he was gay and apparently liked me for more than just a friend. We talked about where I could go so we decided on an empty field in the northern part of Glendora. I fell asleep only to be awoken by Scott and

> If I could give advice to any child in the foster care system today, the first thing I would tell them is to never ever give the okay for any of your foster parents to have guardianship over you. For one thing, you never know if the parents will suddenly change character, as all of mine did, probably because they were no longer under the constant scrutiny of social workers. Another thing, if trouble within that family does ever crop up, getting help from the system will be extremely difficult, if not impossible.

one of his friends looking for me. Scott then took me to his house. So I stayed with him for a week. In the meantime I was still going to school and doing my homework and so on. The following week I got called to the Teacher's Lounge during my Electronics Elective Class. I complained that it was against the rules for students to go to the Teacher's Lounge but I was assured it was okay this one time. When I got there, there was a cop waiting for me. This police officer told me that he had every right to arrest me but he wasn't going to because in all the umpteen years that he ever had to pick up a run away, he had never had one that didn't also run away from school. Never. Not once. So he told me to go home after school and that if I didn't, then he really would arrest me. That afternoon, I went back home. I was dreading it but I did as I was told. When I got there, I saw all my stuff on the curb. Caroline told me to wait by the curb and as I waited, my Electronics Elective teacher, one of my favorite teachers, Mr. Harry Timid, drove up and took me away. I was elated.

The Timid's

SOMETIME IN 1977: C. and H. Timid. I was 17 years old. The staff at Glendora High School realized by now that I was a "troubled teen" and assisted me in finding employment on campus and a counselor give me an MTBI personality test to determine where I would best fit in for current and future employment. The problem was that my personality score was lopsided in a way that she had never seen before. By "lopsided" I mean that of the four functions that are tested, I scored almost zero on two (judgment and intuition) and very highly on the other two (introversion and perception). She made me retake the test and told me to be honest in my answers, but once again my score came out lopsided. I do not understand why they couldn't recognize me

> I am so fortunate I was able to "fall through the cracks" growing up or else I would be on crack.

as autistic back then, even though the state of California had acknowledged autism as a valid diagnosis since 1971, but I guess it was a good thing they didn't, since back then autism was listed as a type of schizophrenia. But what they did do is label me as "emotionally disturbed".

H. told me that I ate too much and needed to cut back on what I ate, despite me still being very underweight (5'10"120#). For six months they both complained about not having enough money to buy enough food. Then all of a sudden "the check came in". They were paid by the state for keeping custody of me, including six months of back pay. So there was more food but . . . nothing changed. I was still given the same portions of food as before. I was still told I was being greedy if I asked for seconds. But there were some things that did change. Harry got a new car. H. got a new stereo. I knew where all the money meant to care for me was going. I lost all respect for H. and C. at that point. My dream foster home was turning into another nightmare and I told my social worker that I didn't want to stay there anymore.

McKinely Home For Boys

SOMETIME IN 1977: I went to live at McKinely Home for Boys. I was a member of the Upward Bound program. I was only capable of going on Upward Bound excursions during the summertime, when school was let out. One of those summers was spent at Berkeley . . . yes, that Berkeley! Our assignment was to develop a term paper. That was it. We were at Berkeley while a professional cheerleading convention was gathered, although I was not interested in any of the cheerleading events, and not because I didn't like good looking women. I mean, just because I was autistic didn't mean I was blind, but I already knew from experience that none of these type of girls would ever like me anyways. In fact, many of them had made fun of me as a child.

I had a crush on a certain black girl who was in my Upward Bound group. All I can remember about her now was she was very cute, had pretty eyes, and seemed very nice. I got up very early in the morning just so I could be around her—and boy did she ever get up very early. One day, on our way back from a local trip, two black football players got on the elevator with me and her on the way back to our room in the campus dorm we were staying in. I felt very nervous and so did she, but I became really nervous when they started flirting with her and telling her what a fine, good looking girl she was. I snuggled up next to her and whispered into her ear, telling her I had a plan to get her away from here and protect her. I pretended to get off on our floor alone but then did a fake and let her run out of the elevator to safety. I realize now that she probably wasn't under danger but it was the thought that counts.

Then I got into trouble. It seems that my thesis paper, while all my own, wasn't exactly what they were looking for. I was supposed to create a thesis paper from scratch, not resubmit a previously submitted thesis paper. So I was boarded on a bus to be sent home alone. As I sat on the bus to be taken away, I looked out the window at the group that was forced to gather and watch me depart, I saw the beautiful black girl crying her eyes out. She was a woman and instead of showing the hate and anger the group leader and some of the other boys were displaying, she was showing her feelings of compassion and I appreciate and respect her for that even today. Only women are like that.

I saw my biological mother at a halfway house. This was an actual house and was full of creepy people. My mother was in a very small room, big enough for only one cot, a toilet, and a sink. My mother sat cross-legged on the cot. My mom and the social worker talked for a long time together and I sat there bored. Then I became very uncomfortable when my mom started smoking and filled the room with smoke. Finally we left but I never really got to talk to my mom. I had one more chance when one of my biological brothers took me to see her again, shortly after I aged out of the orphanage, but when I saw my mom, I couldn't talk to her. My brother told me she was on heroin. Then my brother kept telling me about how he had seen a wet spot on her cot. This grossed me out. I felt that I couldn't have any kind of relationship with a mom like that. In hindsight, I can see how my brother didn't like her. My brother was always talking about how great our biological dad was but I never remember him saying anything good about our mom. I wish I knew and felt the way I do now, back then. My mother and I could have been good for each other because I believe my mother was either autistic or she was autistic-friendly.

I never took a shower in the boy's home and this bothered the administration. They tried forcing me to take a shower one day by making me strip and then watching me get in the shower but gave up because I over-reacted to their request.

I have always hated drugs. I could see what drugs did to other kids. I could see how they would try to escape the pain of reality but it would make them even more vulnerable to pain and abuse then I was as an autistic child. They became zombies or stupid. The drugs became their master instead of them being masters of the drugs. I never criticized or narked on any of the kids who took drugs and they knew that they could trust me in this regard. But I still let them know that I thought taking drugs was very bad for them and they shouldn't abuse themselves like that. You would be surprised how these kids got some of their drugs. In the middle of the campus was a building where a psychiatrist was situated. I went to him one day and he was horrible. Nothing he said helped or comforted me, and he ended our session by prescribing a bottle of little red pills, which I took back to my cottage and took as prescribed. I hated them. They didn't make me feel any better, in fact I felt worse because they made me very groggy. A much younger kid from a different cottage came into my dorm room and told me

> People look to technology or a pill or an authority figure (religious or governmental) to cure whatever ails them. But no matter how wonderful the technology or the pill or the people, it doesn't do anything to make us better people inside. If anything, it makes us worse. It destroys our creative problem solving abilities.
>
> Stay away from any and all prescription drugs meant to modify or improve your behavior. As you are transitioning from a toddler to an adult, you will be diagnosed, misdiagnosed, rediagnosed, and undiagnosed endlessly. Every time you see a new doctor or psychiatrist, your "real problem" will be discovered and the cure will be a prescription drug. Hello? Remember that there is absolutely no cure for Autistic's, so anything they give you will screw up your mind or your body or both, but they will never actually cure you, you will still be "broken". So the end results of all these drugs is 1) they will make the drug companies money, 2) they will justify the doctor's existence (and paycheck), and 3) they will mask (not cure) only a very small subset of your symptoms. Furthermore, these drugs will have side-effects that will need to be masked by yet more drugs and those drugs will have side effects that need to be countered by yet more drugs, and so on ad infinitum. Your life will become worse, not better, but worse yet, the people who are in charge of your care (your parents) will (mis)perceive it as a change for the better. That is because they won't have to deal with you on your level—you will be more passive and uninvolved—a zombie. It is the easy way out for them but at your expense. Don't do it!

he was going to Disneyland. He asked if I wanted to go with him. I said how was that possible? He told me that one of the approved outside "handlers" was given a Suburban and passes to take some of the kids along and because I had been so good to their cottage whenever I "babysitted" them that they wanted me to go with them.

This kid told me that if I sucked the handlers dick that I could make $20—which was a lot of money in a place where there was no money. I asked this kid if he did that and he said lots of kids did it, it was easy money. I told him no thanks. He then asked me what I was doing with the bottle of little red pills and I said I was thinking of throwing them away because I hated them; they made me feel groggy. He asked if he could have them and I said why? He said the little red pills were "the best" and highly sought after in the orphanage but you had to take more than one for them to have any effect. I thought he had been nice to me and, most importantly, very honest with me, so I thought I would be nice to him and let him have the pills. Later on I regretted doing this because I didn't want to help anyone destroy their lives by doing drugs.

Try to remember that as soon as you turn 18, you are an adult. You are then free to make your own decisions and you are free to reject the advice/decision/guidance of other adults around you. You can say no to any and all drugs, for example. Also try to remember that the very same adults who are telling you that whatever decisions they have made for you is only for your good in mind, may try to "force your hand" and threaten to withdraw support, whether that support be in the form of money or government assistance or a place to stay, and so on. This is blackmail and is unethical, from my point-of-view. Having a decision forced upon you is never good, even if the intentions are.

Learning To Drive

I'M GOING TO BREAK format here for a short while to tell a different kind of story. I've heard stories from some parents about their grown-up autistic progeny that couldn't learn to drive. I thought about that and at first, I thought to myself that I never had any problems learning to drive, so how could I relate to that? Driving seems so easy but Autistics are known for thinking and behaving kind of peculiarly, then I gave it some more thought and I realized that I didn't display any problems in Driver's Ed or to the observer who rode gunshot with me so I could get my Driver's License issued to me in California, that I could tell. Yet actually, you see, I did have a problem in Driver's Ed that was very significant, as I will tell you about shortly. That's the problem with blind spots, you can't see them. I had a problem and couldn't tell I had a problem until tens of years later . . .

At the Gestalt's, some older kids who were either friends of Keith and Carrie or they were relatives of the Gestalt's, these kids asked us if we wanted a ride in their car. They had a hopped up Mustang with no seats. The car rumbled and shook when it started up, and the big fat tires in the back would churn and smoke when they took off. So we went for a ride and met up with some other kids who also had a hotrod, only they had an early model Chevy with a big, chromed-out V-8 in it. They both revved their engines at a stop light and when the light turned green, both cars zoomed ahead. Because there were no seats, I was told to sit in back and place my feet on the driver's lower back so he wouldn't slide around on his butt while driving. I couldn't see anything out the windows then but the tops of trees and streetlights. We raced through about three or four lights and then went home. What I learned from this was that everyone appeared to want to race and speed. So . . .

At Driver's ED at Glendora High School, when we went for a drive in the Foothills Mountains, I would drive on the wrong side of the road, cutting corners like a race car because that is what I had seen race cars do. I would watch for approaching cars whenever I made a sharp left turn and then scoot back over to the right lane in adequate time to avoid a collision. It scared the death out of my instructor and a fellow schoolmate who was also learning to drive, but I thought they were either over-reacting or they were pretending.

After I got my driver's license, I remember getting caught driving my '64 Corvair over 90MPH on a long stretch of empty road near Walnut, California. The cop said the only reason he wasn't giving me a ticket was because he didn't know how fast I was driving but he said it scared him because he saw me getting air-time on one of the little hills in the road.

When I first arrived in Phoenix, I bought a second car, a '65 Corvair Corsa 180 that was slightly modified for high performance driving. I didn't have it very long though. I didn't like to drive since I was afraid of my car because it was too fast. I was especially afraid to drive it in rush hour traffic. Then a friend of my roommate insisted I take them to see my roommate after he got out of work because he had no transportation, and it was at the height of rush hour. So I drove him to see my roommate at this work and as I approached an intersection, I saw the light turn yellow, but instead of slowing down, I floored it. I thought it was a fast car so I was supposed to drive it fast. The problem was that there was a driver in the left hand turn lane that was impatient, yet I kept going. As I entered the intersection, the other driver gunned their vehicle into mine. I already changed lanes into the painted crosswalk of the intersection to avoid him, but I still kept going. After he clipped my vehicle, I kept going straight onto the curb, almost hitting a man walking by. The car wasn't exactly totaled but I never fixed it. In fact, I held onto bits and pieces of it (mainly the engine and transaxle), until I couldn't hold onto them anymore when I became homeless and they were repossessed by a towing company. Although I eventually got it back again from a cop, Daryl Parry, who lent me $300 to get it back. I say he "lent" me the money although I never got the opportunity to pay him back for his kindness.

Speaking of Darryl, he also got me a job driving a Toyota Corolla for a mortgage company. At first I tried to obey all the laws and regulations of driving. I wanted to be a safe driver. Well I did learn how to be a safe driver because after my accident in my '65 Corvair, I wanted to avoid accidents. The only problem I had was doing the speed limit. The I-10 along Mesa, Arizona, used to be a four-lane highway with thick oleanders dividing the lanes. I would drive along this highway, doing exactly 55MPH and people would honk and flip me off, just because I was doing the speed limit. Everyone was doing 65 MPH, which was 10 miles over the speed limit. I had no idea why people had no respect for the law but I thought if they had no respect for the law, and it was their law, why should I respect it too then? So I decided screw it, and I drove as fast as I pleased from then on. I would do 100+ MPH on the highway on a regular basis. Well that is, until I was much older and learned that people, in general, only think about what is inconvenient for them to do, like stop at a light that just turned red when you are speeding and they don't value being reasonable, courteous, or prudent towards each other.

I had a roommate (I think his name was Terry) that drove a custom VW. It wasn't really fast, but it wasn't slow and it handled very well. He offered to let me drive his car if I let him drive my car (I had another Corvair, this one a '69 coupe). When I was driving his car, he told me not to act so "stiff", and play around and get a feel for the way his car really handled. So I did what I was told. I was all over the road, swerving left and right, right in front of a cop coming at us from the other direction. I saw the cop but payed no heed until the cop turned on his emergency lights and my roommate panicked and told me to stop and he expressed fear at getting caught. I told him not to worry, dodged down a side street, made a U-turn and parked the car by the curb of a house. I told him to hunch down so he couldn't be seen and turned off the car. The cops drove by, shined their spotlight at the car, and drove away. I told my roommate to stay down still, that they would be making a second pass in a few minutes, but if we hurried, we could get out of the car and take a walk before they returned, which they did, and when they left the second time, I told my roommate it was safe to leave. He never let me drive his car again.

Another time, I had another roommate in my car. We were driving around in circles looking for a 7-11, when we passed by an old couple driving too slowly, then we doubled-back and saw them on the other side of the road in the left-turn lane. My roommate said he wish he could really give them something to be scared of so they would get off the streets and never drive again. He said would it be funny if, since they were directly opposite us across an intersection in the left hand turn lane, that when the light turned green, someone would zoom up to their car and blocked their way so they couldn't turn. I thought okay, so I did it but wouldn't you know it, a cop turned up. The cop asked me why I did it and I said because my roommate suggested that I do so, and amazingly, the cop let me go with just a warning.

In 2001 I got a Honda S2000. I loved this car but I didn't like the way the Torsen rear axle acted like a straight axle so that whenever I "burned rubber", both wheels would always spin together—that meant no traction at the rear whatsoever whenever this happened. Other than that, the S2000 was a very high quality car. It was also very fast. I don't mean it was the fastest car in the world, but it was faster than most. It could get you speeding tickets real fast too, which is exactly what I did. I was doing over 75 in a 45 MPH zone. Nowadays, that is a serious crime but I got away with a misdemeanor. That was the last time I ever tried to speed. I had averaged a speeding ticket once every two years until that time and since then I haven't received a speeding ticket. I have finally "mellowed out" I guess you could say.

Almost On My Own

SEPTEMBER, 1978: ON THE recommendation of a houseparent at McKinely's, I enrolled in BIOLA (The Bible Institute of Los Angeles) to major in communications. This was crazy, seeing as I had already enrolled in Cal Poly for an electronic engineering degree. It was a mistake, but not as big as it might seem, seeing as I was deathly afraid of being in a dorm with other people. While I was at BIOLA, my worst nightmares played out. I was not comfortable around other people and many of them didn't treat me very well. Students had to pick two after-school electives and I chose proselytizing in the local Jewish community of Los Angeles. I dreaded this because I had to physically go door-to-door and talk to people I didn't know. It was awful, but not as awful as my second elective: a news announcer for the on-campus radio station. As a highly introverted and withdrawn loner, this was not a good thing. Naturally I didn't last long but before I dropped out at the end of December 1978, I wrote an article to the editor and told them what I felt. This is a copy of what I had written:

To the Editor:

I saw Jesus the other day—in person! He was walking up the street towards the cafeteria. But he wasn't His usual self. There was sadness in His face. I watched as tears came to His eyes. Looking around me, I could see why He was sad. I saw people cutting in line, I saw guys staring lustfully at girls or trying to impress them, I saw some people holding up the line as they selfishly took two or three plates of food while others looked hungrily on, I saw people sitting alone at tables stuffed with people in their own little clique, and I saw phony Christians trying to act righteous and waiting for the right moment to attack a humbled or sacrificing Christian.

I looked back at Jesus though, and I could see that that wasn't what bothered Him. His pain evidently came from what they were saying to excuse their actions: "Nobody's perfect", "I'm in a hurry!", "But I'm hungry!", "Don't worry, nobody will care. They're all Christians too! They're supposed to be self-sacrificing!", "They'll forgive me", "Mind your own business, you hypocrite! You're no better!", "We aren't saved by our good works", and on and on.

I heard spiritually fat Christians who were living off the Word of God only for their own good, and not for others. Sure they all love God, but they love themselves, their cars, their stereos, their stomachs, their love life, and their money even more.

"Then why do you think I'm going to Biola? Why should I sacrifice my weekend for my CS? Why all these sacrifices when I could be going to UCLA or better, instead of here?", they say. Well the answer is, "I don't know", because they are the same people who also said, "We aren't saved by our good works". They say one thing and live another while showing their ignorance of Scripture because the Bible says we aren't saved by good works alone, but by faith in Jesus the Messiah. The life of love and mercy is made more spiritual by the law of good works. We are saved by God's mercy and love and our lifestyles (Jews vs Gentile, Black vs White, rich vs poor, rock n roll vs Christian Music Freaks, etc) mean nothing! Love knows no barriers because love can melt all those barriers down to reveal the real person inside all of us.

Who's to say whether I ever really saw Jesus—especially in person? I'll tell you how I saw Him. I saw Him in the eyes of a girl who said "Hi" to me when I was lonely and homely looking. I saw Him in the eyes of a guy who let someone cut in front of him without saying a word or looking angry, I saw Him in the eyes of a person who let someone in front of him grab two plates of food while his own stomach grumbled but his mouth didn't, I saw Him in the eyes of a person who hated to be left out of a clique but was more then willing to carry away all the dishes they "forgot" to clean-up. That's where I saw Jesus. But the thing that really gets me is, why didn't anyone else see Him?

Andrew J Robinson
Freshman, Communications
Published in The Chimes, Dec 1, 1978

My ex-foster brother who lived with me at the Hippos' helped me find a place to stay by inviting me to room with him and a gay man. The foster brother said that he himself wasn't gay, but in hindsight this was a lie. My foster brother had all kinds of gay friends that he hung out with or lived with at one time or another. While many of his gay friends gave me "the eye", they never bothered me too much.

I found a job washing dishes at a local Marie Calendars. I then saved up enough money to buy myself a 1964 Corvair Monza from Scott Kostca's mom for $300. Although I understood how automobiles functioned, I had no experience maintaining them or fixing them and I didn't know how to apply my knowledge in a practical manner. What I didn't understand was that cars had to be registered. At least I had a car to get around in.

Then my boss told me something about getting a certain unexpected job done before closing time or I would have to stay until

> While I don't hate gays, I have never had any good experiences with them and if you've noticed, I've had quite a few interactions with gays growing up: at the orphanages, in school, and at home. I believe that the vulnerable and naïve nature of Autistics appeals to quite a few gay men, who then try to exploit this quality for their benefit. Men, gay or straight, do not make good lovers like women do and I find men sexually disgusting because of this. It also makes me feel sorry for women in general because of the limited choices they have in finding a truly loving mate or lover.

one-in-the-morning (my normal hours were to five pm). He talked and acted like I was in trouble. I was scared and had no idea why he said what he did so I walked out . . . actually I ran out and while I was running out, I accidentally brushed up against the breasts of one of the waitresses. I went home but returned the next day to try and apologize to the waitress by waiting outside after working hours. She got into her car and I walked up to her and as soon as she saw me she started honking her horn at me. My boss told me he was just joking but I didn't believe him.

The Marine Corps

Before aging out of McKinely Home for Boys, they had put lots of pressure on me to join the military. They asked what was I going to do and where was I going to live after I aged out. I told them I didn't know but I would figure it out. If they really wanted to help me, they would help me figure out what to do too. I told them the last thing I wanted to do was go from a boy's home into a men's home, which is exactly what I thought of the military at that time. But after quitting Marie Calendar's, that's when I decided to try and join the military anyway. I wanted to join the Air Force but no one in the recruit office would talk to me except for the USMC (United States Marine Corps), so I joined them. I took the ASVAB test and apparently scored so high that I qualified for an officer position without having to have a college degree as was per the normal qualifications. They said that the State of California would sponsor me in officer school or something like that. I had problems keeping my '64 Corvair running so I gave it away because I figured I wouldn't need it in the military. Of course, there was that little problem of me wetting my bed. I was in the MCRD (Marine Corp Recruit Depot) for nine weeks before being "discovered". As part of my punishment, I was forced to take my wet sheets to an atrium that existed between the two barracks, and wash them by hand where everyone could see me. This was a case of Deja Vu. As if that wasn't humiliating enough, the Drill Sergeants and recruits started taunting me. So I started taunting them back. I called one of the Drill Sergeants a bad name, and when he threatened to kick my ass, I told him to go ahead and bring his fat ass down here and try it. I started cussing out and insulting all the Drill Sergeants and the next thing I knew I heard the slam and click of all the windows on the barracks being closed. My own Drill Sergeant came down and did his Drill Sergeant thing and I just ignored him and gave him attitude. I'm sure I must have shocked him to death. I mean me: the "shy", "wimpy" little kid that wasn't acting at all shy or wimpy anymore. He asked me if I wanted to go to the Brigg (military prison) and I said of course not and he said that's where I would be going if I didn't act right. What was I going to say to the review board he asked? I said, the truth, that the Drill Sergeants were humiliating me and encouraging the entire platoon to join in with them. So he changed his attitude and suddenly was the nicest man you could ever meet. He asked me what the problem was and I told him how stupid could he be? I was being humiliated and he had the nerve to ask me what my problem was? He said in times of war a person could be put under a lot of stress and my survival could depend on tolerating stress just like all the other recruits. I told him I understood that but this was more than just a war time exercise because if I ever graduated from there, I would be joining my fellow recruits in the adult world and living with these people, people who would humiliate me and make fun of me for the rest of my life. I had enough of that growing up. The Drill Sergeant acknowledged that, said he would see what he could do to help me and then went back into character. I took the sheets back in and I was never humiliated the rest of the time I was there.

The Marines tried monitoring me at night by making me get up once an hour and watching me take a pee. Incredibly this didn't work at stopping me from wetting my bed. So they let me go. I got an honorable discharge without benefits, but not before I sneaked a peak at one of their evaluation sheets of me. This is what the Marine Corps thought of me . . .

UNRELIABLE				SOMETIMES
WISE GUY				SOMETIMES
PHYSICAL WEAKLING				A LITTLE
SAD/DEPRESSED				SOMETIMES
MARCHING SKILL		X		
MANUAL OF ARMS			X	

KNOWLEDGE				X	
CO-ORDINATION			X		
ENDURANCE		X			
WILLINGNESS TO WORK				> <	

". . . below avg. Going downhill. Will keep an eye on him."

". . . he has no discipline . . ."

". . . is way too shy . . . seems to live in his own world . . . he is quiet but good . . ."

". . . is becoming salty in his last days in MCRD . . ."

". . . he is a wimp . . ."

". . . he is starting to get himself into a lot of trouble. He just exists in the platoon. Very unmotivating . . ."

I know the Marines talk all about finding "a few good men" and I understand I didn't meet their standard, but what I don't understand is why the Drill Sergeants and the recruits all seemed to hate me—and don't tell me they didn't when they said such hateful things to me about me wetting my bed. Don't get me wrong, the USMC was a great experience for me to have to go through. They taught me the value of pain, that pain was feedback, not something you always need to avoid or run away from. They taught me how to deal with authorities in a respectful manner that made interactions with them go more smoothly. I was taught the value of self-discipline (the ability to do what needs to be done without having someone have to tell you to do it). I learned the value of teamwork but I also learned that I was never going to be a part of any team or group, ever. And believe it or not, they taught me how to walk. Autistics are known for walking funny, but I walk like a Marine, which doesn't look so funny.

I tend to avoid eye contact because I don't want to feel what you are feeling. It is like the only time I can really feel anything is when I look at you. Yet when I look away, the feeling goes away. It is like this because it really isn't my feeling, it is your feeling. So it can be uncomfortable or even scary to look at you and feel your emotions and not mine. I can't have my own emotions when I look at you. If you hate me, I feel your hate. I cannot feel neutral or angry or happy, I can only feel your hate. Why would I want to have your feelings and not mine, even your good ones? It is better not to look. It is very stressful to live in a world full of someone else's emotions. But I learned from the USMC that even under great stress, amazingly you can still function, and boy was I ever in stress in the USMC. I mean, here I was, under stress all the same as all the other recruits, but with the additional stress of trying to get away with not getting caught wetting my bed almost every single night for nine weeks. Yet I could adequately function and keep up with all the other recruits. I believe that some children with autism can handle the stress of being autistic and others cannot handle it and they buckle up and shut down.

One little strategy that really works well for me to handle stress is to completely or mostly withdraw, that way I can avoid any interaction. The question becomes then, how much stress can I take on with all my different strategies? That is a dangerous and unpleasant question, but I've been there and back many times through no fault of my own. No one can be a superhuman so although I can function with the stress of autism (as can your autistic children if taught properly), I don't push my limits. I mainly try to minimize my stress at all times but there are times I sacrifice my comfort for the comfort of others.

The Rest Of The Story

Sometime in 1979: After being discharged from the Marines, I did two things: I signed up to go to DeVry in Phoenix, Arizona and I snuck back to the Timid's because I had nowhere else to go. I lied to the Timid's and told them I just graduated from the USMC and was awaiting transfer orders. I used that as an excuse so they would let me stay there the one or two months I needed before DeVry started a new semester. I then left for DeVry in Phoenix and I immediately found a job working as a janitor at Arizona Eastern Star Home. I rented a room from an old lady but I was depressed and unmotivated to study so I quickly dropped out of Devry. The place I worked at as a janitor was owned by the Masons and when new management took over, they laid me off because I wasn't a member of the Masons and the jobs at the retirement complex were reserved for members of the Masons.

I found another job right away working at a very small company (less than 10 people total) called Gardiner Electronics. Mr. Gardiner manufactured metal detectors. They didn't have the "polish" of what a big professional company with lots of resources could put out, but they worked and certain people loved them. I did various fill in jobs, but mainly I did the PCB (printed circuit board) layouts.

Now that I had a job and a place to live, I had to stock my refrigerator. Well actually, it wasn't MY refrigerator, as I shared an apartment with three other guys. I had no idea what I needed or should buy so I got what I knew I liked: jelly beans and milk. I eventually got tired of jelly beans and milk so I upgraded to bologna and cheese slices and milk.

I was at a McDonald's and one of my many long strings of roommates and I was watching a pretty girl bending over while sweeping and cleaning the floor. She was wearing tight pants and bent right over in front of us and my roommate whispered something about how he would like to grab her in the crotch/ass, and I thought that sounded like a good idea. I got in big trouble for that. The whole restaurant erupted into chaos and they were all yelling at me.

I thought I could learn to cook my own meals, I mean how hard could it be? I took a cooking class in High School but my classmates wouldn't let me do anything by myself; they would do everything for me. We did everything in groups and I'm surprised I even passed this class. I had been to cookouts and it looked easy. So I went to the supermarket and . . . well . . . I didn't know what to pick out. There were so many types of steaks and how was I supposed to know the difference between all of them? I recognized the name of one them, T-bone, so I picked that. I took it home and stuck it in the freezer until I was ready to cook it, then I took it out and placed it bare naked on a brand new skillet I had just bought. I couldn't figure out what setting to put the flame at so I turned it all the way up. At first, nothing appeared to be happening but I then I started to notice that the kitchen was getting smoky, but where was the smoke coming from? It didn't appear to be coming from the steak. I tried turning the steak over so it would cook evenly but I couldn't get the steak off of the skillet. Using extreme force, I finally got the steak off of the skillet but pieces of it were permanently stuck. I didn't know how long it took to cook a steak or how to tell if it was done. When I finally got the rest of the steak off of the skillet, it was horrible. The outside was burnt and the inside was freezing cold and rare. The skillet was ruined.

Then I lost my job at Gardiner Electronics. So now I had nothing. I had no job, no place to live, and of course, being autistic, I had no friends, and being an orphan I had no one else to turn to. I also didn't have a car anymore I had to walk an average of eight miles a day, looking for a job to keep me alive. As I passed by any fast food restaurant, I would stop and go in and fill out a job application. There were a few problems with this though. I had no contact number or home address. They would ask how they could contact me and I told them I would drop by again in a couple of days. They asked where I was going to live and I told them the same place I was living now: out in the street. If I got a job I would find places nearby for me to stay at until I got enough money to get my own place. They said no way. They didn't like the way I looked and they didn't like the way I smelled. To make things worse, I heard a comedian joke about when they asked him for his "Sex?" in a job application, he would cross out the "M" and "F" and put "Yes", so I thought this would be something funny to put on my job application too. I thought people would find it amusing but I was wrong. They were very offended instead.

One of my favorite places to sleep at night was the front door steps of a church, any church. Vagrants and homeless people never went to places like that, so I felt safe. Sometimes, not knowing what day of the week it was, I would be woken up by a church-goer who came in early to prepare the church for services that morning. None of these people ever offered me help, a few even threatened to call the police even though I said or did nothing to them; they were just scared of me. I went to a Catholic church one day and asked two priests who were closing down for the day, if I could sleep on the front steps of their church and they said no way. I then asked these two priests if they could spare a dollar and they said they had no money but that if I was hungry and needed shelter, I could go to a local charity. I asked them if one of them could give me a ride there since it was far from where we were at that time and they said sorry, they were in no position to help me. I always thought this was interesting. Priests had no obligation to help or make sacrifices for others. They would preach about helping the poor and destitute yet they themselves did nothing about it other than to tell others to do something about it. It wasn't their job, it was somebody else's within the Catholic organization.

I knew that I was naïve by nature and therefore vulnerable. People told me so all the time and I knew it was true, I just didn't know why or how I was like that. Even today, many people will talk down to me like I am a little kid. I just couldn't "grow up", no matter how hard I tried. Nevertheless, I didn't want to take chances. I stayed as far away as I could from local homeless charities. I heard terrible stories about those places. I heard that bikers frequented those places as recruiters, looking to persuade victims for various "jobs". I would have no protection from predators at these places. They had work but it was outdoors doing yard-work and I still had problems with my asthma.

For food, I found that if I had a dollar and bought a burrito at a 7-11, the burrito would quickly disappear and I would be even hungrier than before, even if I had another burrito or two after that. But I discovered by accident one day, that if I ate a candy bar, then had a burrito, I would be completely satisfied.

An older couple, some Mennonites in Sunnydale, took me in for a short time, under the condition that I went to their Mennonite services. I went to a gathering at the home of one of the staff members at their church and got into trouble because when they gathered together to socialize, the men were all in one part of the home and the women were all in another part of the home. I could get along better with women, and women were more interesting to talk to than men, so I joined the women, not realizing that I was the only man present in the room. The staff member was very offended by this and told me what I did was wrong, but I couldn't understand why they segregated and discriminated against women so I argued with him about the morality of his belief, which resulted in me being sent home early.

I returned to the Arizona Eastern Star Home I used to work at one night because I thought maybe the old people there would have pity on me and give me a dollar or two but I was wrong. They told me to get lost. It was late at night and I decided that I would sleep behind a parking curb in the nearly empty parking lot. Well, one of the old folks reported this to security and security came out and arrested me. They then called the police. The cop (Daryl Parry) turned out to be a very nice person who helped me out when I was caught loitering. He was a lieutenant in the Police Reserves and was an executive manager at Margaretten & Company, Inc. a mortgage company that needed a "runner"—a person who would drive a company car around and deliver loan papers and such. Daryl helped me find a place to live and gave me some food to stock my home with. Daryl got laid off one day and then he took off to California and I never saw or heard of him again. Daryl was one of the extremely few men in my life that I was able to respect. Daryl was a good man.

Sometime in 1984: **Advanced Diagnostic Research**. I was 24 years old. There was a co-worker here, named Mike, who was a bodybuilder and I tried to be friends with him. I thought he could show me how to take care of myself and show me how to be better looking. So one day he told me he could show me how to become a bodybuilder too, took me to this Gym, and had me lift the heaviest weights I could find and exercise all parts of my body. Well, anyone who has ever studied the physiology of exercise knows that that is the worst thing you can do. This man was not my friend. He had a cruel streak in him and was being hateful by doing that to me. I had done too much too soon and you can't feel injuries to your muscle at the time you injure them, there is a delay of about two days. The result was, two days later I was very sore all over, but especially in my calves. My calves even got to the point where they cramped up so I had to walk on my tiptoes. Of course, Mike thought this was hilarious. That's how "good-hearted" of a person he was. Unfortunately, I was just beginning to learn that there are lots of Mike's out there in the real world.

There was this woman at ADR who told me I was autistic and I didn't believe her. All I knew about autistic people was that they were mentally retarded and they abused themselves. I was or did neither, so how could I be autistic? I thought she was trying to insult me by saying that. I can understand now that autism was for the longest time (up until 1980), considered a form of schizophrenia.

I met this black woman bodybuilder at ADR. I thought a bodybuilder woman would be all masculine and cartoonish looking like male bodybuilders are, but I was wrong. She was very feminine looking, with a tight little waist and firm-looking legs, butt, and chest. The only thing that gave her away was her neck and her arms—well at least when she flexed them. But I thought she was very attractive other than that.

Sometime in 1986: **Motorola**. I was 26 years old. I met a co-worker here who appeared to be a black man and his name was John McDaniels. When I went to his home, I saw that his whole family was Mexican and not black, so I asked him, did your mom have an affair with a black postman/milkman or something? He told me that he was from Puerto Rico and there were a lot of people like him; they were a mixed race and every so often a black child would be born into the families. He mentioned some derogatory name that they call those children but I don't remember what it was. So I said he must be very lucky because he had the best of both worlds: he was a black and he was a Mexican and he could be accepted by both sides without prejudice. He said, "No Andrew, I have the worst of both worlds: Mexicans hate me because I look black and blacks hate me because they know I'm Mexican and I speak Spanish and eat Spanish food". I immediately had strong feelings for this man because I knew his pain of never being able to fit in through no fault of your own. I did not judge him because he had served prison time for armed robbery. He was muscular from working out as a Golden Gloves Boxer. I saw a man whom I wanted to be like when I "grew up" someday.

John McDaniels taught me what it was like to dance. To the great annoyance of people around me, I was constantly drumming my hands and fingers rhythmically against everything I touched. John said that I had a rhythm and rhythm was the key to dancing, only instead of using my hands and fingers, I could use other parts of my body and instead of making my own rhythm, I could use the rhythm of the music. Eventually I developed this into what I call "stimming to the beat". I still "stim to the beat" quite often and this is the reason why I do so.

I was living in a rented house with some roommates and they suggested that if I wanted a girlfriend, I needed to get out and the best place to do that was a bar. I picked a bar I could dance at (Bobby McGee's) since I loved to stim to the beat . . . I mean dance. I didn't know what else to do. I just sat around in the bar drinking coke, even though I didn't like coke, because they had no chocolate milk. I didn't talk with anyone and I just stared at the people dancing on the dance floor. I didn't know what to do and I couldn't carry on much of a conversation with anyone. Then these two gay guys asked me to join their group, so I did. I didn't know they were gay and I wouldn't have cared anyway, but in hindsight I know this wasn't a socially smart thing to do. In hindsight, after I started suspecting they were gay, I should have stopped hanging out with them because I didn't realize that if I wanted to meet women, hanging out with gay guys was not a socially intelligent thing to do because the women would assume I was gay because I hung out with gay guys.

One of the gay guys took me to see an escort so that I would no longer be "troubled by being a virgin". Somehow this was supposed to change me into "a real man" or something like that. But it had no effect on my personality whatsoever. I went to see her on my own afterwards. She was a beautiful and sexy woman and I told her so. She said, "Let's fuck" and I said no, let's not. I said I wanted her to take the time and show me what it would take to please a woman, so if I ever got a girlfriend I could take care of her needs. She said she didn't know how to do that and I said it didn't matter, all she had to do was tell me what she wanted and how she liked it, and I could practice listening and responding. But there is one thing I wanted her to work with

> What is the difference between having sex and making love? I have never met one man who ever knew the difference. Men always equate having sex with making love. They aren't even close. Women in general are treated like trophies or blow-up sex dolls, not like fellow human beings with feelings. Very few people can even define love in a way that makes sense. Scientists who study these kinds of things call it "affectional systems" and not love per se.

me first, and that was to tell me how she liked to receive cunnilingus. So I paid $50 for half-an-hour and she gave me an hour. She even took the phone off the hook. She was the first woman I ever had sex with. Afterwards, while we were getting dressed, I took a look at the pictures on her wall and I saw she had a son, so I asked her how her son was doing and what he was like and where was he. I think this woman liked me because she followed me out the door and waved bye to me on the balcony of the apartment she was at until I was out of sight.

Yet I still got "lucky". It wasn't long before I met a friend of a friend of theirs, Mary E Gibson. She had a BS in psychology and she immediately liked me for some reason. This was the start of an eight year relationship. In hindsight, I suppose she liked me because, having studied psychology, she probably recognized that I was autistic and so maybe I fascinated her. Whatever. I tried my best to be good to her, including sexually, and for eight years she was happy. That was the longest relationship either one of us had ever had.

Our relationship wasn't always good. Sometimes we would get into arguments, and I am not good at handling arguments, emotionally speaking. I would have temper tantrums when we got into arguments and throw things. I smashed a couple of wax figurines I had bought her. I threw them down on the kitchen floor and pieces went flying everywhere. She was shocked but I was like "what'd you expect?". I mean, isn't that the point of arguing and fighting? I could never handle aggression very well.

Mary and I would go on camping trips, but I never did well on camping trips. I was always in a bad mood for some reason. I mean a very bad mood. I have always liked being by myself and the only exception I made was for my girlfriends. I had a hard time understanding why they always wanted to go out and do things when I was a homebody and I liked staying home and doing "nothing". If I had known I was autistic, maybe I would have done something different about it. Well, at least I would have tried to be more understanding and considerate of her needs, knowing that we weren't really compatible because I was autistic and had to make more of an effort to "make things work".

The end of our relationship came eight years later when Mary decided she needed to go out and "sow her oats". She left, married a man who allegedly abused her, had a daughter, and then divorced him—all in the space of a few years. She came looking for me one day at lunchtime at my place of work and brought her daughter along with her. She claimed that she thought her daughter maybe had been sexually abused by her ex-husband and that I would be good for her daughter, to help her "recover". She said I needed "one of these" (a daughter) to complete my life. She said I needed to leave that "Chinese bitch" of mine behind and come with her and move to North Dakota. I thought what the Hell was going on and she said yeah, she was all packed up and ready to leave right now. Sure enough, her little pickup with its camper shell was filled to the brim inside with boxes and things. She said she had a job lined up and everything. She said with our combined incomes, we could make a good living together. I told her she had never met my wife so how could she know she was a no-good bitch? Well, I guess I did say a few things about my wife to her, whenever Mary would call me at work, but I didn't think anything I said would have warrantied her calling her a good-for-nothing bitch. I declined the offer and Mary took off, crying.

April of 1987: **EF Data.** The executive secretary at EF Data, a woman named Sandy, had compassion on me and got me going at EF Data. I started out as an assembler, moved up as a Technician, then became—get this—I became a Customer Service Representative. Go figure. I was autistic and I was a Customer Service Representative! Talk about the Peter Principle in action, this has got to take the cake.

I remember going to London for EF Data as a Customer Service Representative. I got to the Heathrow Airport for my flight back to America a couple of hours too early so I started stimming by pacing. I stayed as far away from other people as I could while I was doing it. I was weaving in and out of stores and curtains and various other places trying to avoid people while I was stimming. Airport security started following me around and took me into a room. One of the men held an Uzi while the other man asked me if I was afraid of the other man holding the Uzi and I said I wouldn't be afraid unless he pointed it at me. We talked a little bit and then he let me go. I guess they thought I was a little bit strange and in hindsight, I guess I can't blame them for thinking that.

One of my co-workers was a female JW (Jehovah's Witness) and she invited me to her congregation and a "Bible study". After having a "Bible study" with her for some time, she told me I had to find my own congregation to go to but the first one I went to tried to force me to join another Bible study so I walked out. I went to a different congregation and mentored under an Elder there. While I was studying there, he said I couldn't date non-JW women but then I found out I couldn't date what few JW women were available because none of them would trust me until I had been established as a JW for quite a few years. I thought this disconcerting but I accepted it and continued to study. Part of being a JW meant that I had to go door-to-door and proselytize. This was a very hard thing for me to do but it became extremely hard to do when I found out that no one wanted to go out with me and help me proselytize, yet they still expected me to "put in my hours". Well, needless to say, I didn't feel very wanted or needed or loved by this group so when my Elder was promoted to a different congregation—actually just a change in shifts for that group—everyone assumed I was going to continue to mentor under that Elder, but we had never discussed what I was going to do with this change, so I quietly stopped going. It took them a month before they realized that I wasn't going anymore and two of the Elders called me and asked what was going on. They said they were concerned about me and loved me, so I asked him if that were true, why didn't they notice I was gone for over a month before realizing I had stopped going to any meetings? I told him he was a damn liar and he had nothing to say in reply.

Another one of my co-workers was a Pakastani man, Waheed. No one wanted to be friends with him and it was no wonder, he was plainly anti-American. I "didn't know any better" and tried to be his friend anyways (really I did it because my boss asked me to make friends with him). Of course I had never really had any friends before and it wasn't long before we went our separate ways but before we did, something very significant happened between us. You see, Farhad was not married but neither was he single. His parents, as was per tradition, had prearranged his marriage for him when he was only about eight years old. In Farhad's case, it gets even better for his parents had arranged for him to have two potential wives. All he had to do is choose which one. For Farhad, this meant his parents were no ordinary parents, they were different; they were "better" than most parents were. But I was mystified. Farhad had never met his potential mates before and I asked him, "What if they were both ugly as dogs?". What Farhad told me was very profound. He told me that in Pakistan, dogs were very dirty and disgusting animals. Dogs were never kept as a pet, that was unthinkable, but after being in America for these last few years, he thought he could understand America's love affair with dogs. Dogs were very loyal. They would wait for you to return home and when you got home, no matter what kind of day you had or what kind of mood you were in, they would wag their tail for you and greet you like royalty. They would even defend you to the death. How could you not love an animal like that? Having no idea where their tongue had been, Americans would still let that dog lick them in the face even. Yet no woman is literally as ugly as a dog and if she had a good heart, no matter how "ugly" she was, she would become the most beautiful woman in the world to you (. . . "Hmmm", I thought to myself, "If every day I came home and my wife was wagging her tail for me" . . .). Farhad told me that I didn't have the benefit of having loving parents that knew me better than I knew myself and could pick out the "perfect woman" for me, but he said he thought that I would be a good match for the oriental woman like those at EF Data.

Farhad was right and I took his advice to heart. I decided then and there that I was going to marry a traditional Chinese woman and to do that, I had to learn to speak Chinese and go to China. So I got a book, TEACH YOURSELF CANTONESE, and I learned to speak

Cantonese in nine months. A Chinese man I who had befriended me, Mr. Wong, told me about a 70+ year old woman, Ms. Leung, who needed help learning English so she could get her citizenship. It just so happened that Ms. Leung also had a friend back in China who was looking for a husband and she had promised her that she would find her one when she got to America. I accepted her offer. Thus in December of 1991, I went to China. I had never been on an airplane before or even to an airport, so this was a completely different and new experience for me. I had packed all my belongings a week ahead of time and I lived out of my suitcase at home, just to be sure that I had packed exactly what I needed for a long trip. It was a four week long vacation so I had to be sure of myself. The flight to China was 16 hours long and a little bit scary. To save money, I booked the flight in economy class. The seats were very close together and there was little room to turn around in. We were married while I was in China and have been together ever since.

During the Nagano Olympics, EF Data supplied some 155-Mbs modems to a customer there that needed to use them to support the first overseas HDTV broadcast ever. Unfortunately they didn't know how to get the modems to work when they arrived. These modems were installed in large racks and so could only be repaired on site, so I was sent to help. My escorts, a woman and a man, were preparing to stay for the day and getting things set up so they could be comfortable there for a few days. After half-an-hour I told them I was done. All of their modems were up and running, fully connected to their satellite network. They were completely shocked. I thought they would be very happy but instead they were completely shocked. Did I really fix them? Was the satellite link really working? Yes. I didn't understand their shock but it must have been extreme because the next day they took me by bullet train to the south of Japan to the Mitsubishi plant to see an executive (CEO?) there and explain how I possibly could have fixed their equipment so quickly within half-an-hour of arriving in Nagano. Being autistic I had no idea how politically sensitive the situation like this could be but I told them everything they needed to know. I wanted to be helpful and help them understand how I could do what I did so quickly and accurately. I told them all the things I reasonably saw wrong with the form, fit, and function of the modems. Of course I got in big trouble for this and management told me to never talk to anyone in management of another company while traveling but of course that didn't happen and I was continually in trouble because it was easy to talk me into "spilling the beans" because I wasn't thinking politically, I was thinking of being open and honest and helpful.

In the meantime, my Japanese escort decided that I needed to get drunk. I never understood this custom and I still don't understand this custom. Every time I go to an Asian country, the people there always want to get me drunk. The problem is I rarely drink alcohol. I don't like the taste of alcohol and I don't like the way it makes me feel. I also don't smoke and I am not a male slut but apparently lots of my fellow Americans who travel on international business are and do these kinds of things. I don't know if they were disappointed or impressed by my lack of "vices". I mean they would say I was a "good person" but then they tried to get me drunk or do or say strange things. This time in Japan was no exception. I was taken to their headquarters in Tokyo and they lined up all the female co-workers there and asked me to pick one to be my new escort. So I did. I thought this was cool because I was told to pick the prettiest one but when I did and tried to take her with me, they laughed and said they were just joking.

Afterward, my female escort told me that we weren't taking a taxi this time to get to my hotel, we were walking. What this woman then proceeded to do was take me to every bar from there to my hotel. Apparently there is a custom in Japan where you can walk through the bar and as you walk through it, you hold out exact change for a very small glass of warm Saki and yell out "Wasabi" or something that I can't remember. The bartender would always be waiting to take your money and hand you the glass of Saki and even though I didn't like alcohol, it was easy to swig a small glass of Saki so fast you couldn't even taste it. Besides, it was cold outside and the Saki was warm. We must have gone through about 10 bars before we arrived at my hotel. I felt fine until I said my goodbyes and tried to walk away. My legs didn't cooperate. I thought there must be something wrong with my legs but I couldn't figure out what. I told my escort that something was wrong with my legs and she said I was drunk. I couldn't believe it.

I had never been drunk my whole entire life and this one woman managed to do it with no problem.

In the meantime, I was teaching myself how to program in Assembly Language. I loved computers and programming was fascinating and rewarding to me. I had no employment in this regard so I created a project to develop a programming language of my own: XYZ. I registered a copyright for it, TX4-122-795, on October 18th, 1995. I loved developing this language. I learned how transcendental functions are calculated to any level of precision using primitive calculations and algorithms based on the Taylor or MacLauren series, and continued fractions, and all these equations could be turned into recursive functions. The mnemonics of XYZ were simple and therefore easy to remember, and the syntax was rigid so as to force developers to publish code that was uniformly formatted. Unfortunately it was a DOS program and I never updated it for the Windows graphic environment, although when I retire someday (if I can retire), I will update it so it will support the 64-bit version of the Windows GUI. But I did write a program for Karen in customer service at EF Data, which graphically demonstrated how QPSK, 8PSK, and Vector Modulation worked. This was a very difficult concept for customers to understand and my program made it marvelously simple. When my manager saw how well I could program, he offered to let me help him put together a database for customer service in 1997 . . . and what a database it turned out to be! Everyone who had to work with the database walked away impressed. Even the SGS ISO-9001 inspector said that my database was "outstanding".

While serving as a database administrator at EF Data, I came to work and my manager announced that we were screwed because the IT department had lost 6 months' worth of data due to the tape backup not working and nobody noticing it wasn't working. But I had been making weekly backups of my own for the customer service database ever since I created that database and therefore Customer Service only lost a few days of data. I was almost the hero and would have been rewarded for my foresight, except a few days later a coworker was retiring and sent out an email to everyone, an email which ended in "God bless you", to which I replied to everyone with, "Which God would you be referring to?". This upset some of the religious people there so this one bad event erased all my many good events.

May of 2001: **General Dynamics**. I was 41 years old. After being laid off from EF Data, I went to work at General Dynamics. My very first months spent there was helping my assigned team get on their feet. They had a major problem with getting their high wattage power supplies working. It was a redesign and the engineers couldn't get a handle on it. My supervisor asked me why, as a Senior level technician, why wasn't I getting these issues resolved and I told him because my hands were tied and I could only do what the engineers told me to do. He said let's make a deal and I said I could have everything up and running within three days. I did it in one day. That was ten power supplies that the engineers assigned to this project could not resolve in the two weeks they had worked on it. No product could ship until then. Did I get any recognition for this achievement? No, because I went around saying things like, "How could a technician know more than an engineer?" and "Why don't engineers know basic troubleshooting techniques?". I was just being honest but they were insulted. Of course, I didn't resolve all the problems with the power supplies, only enough to get the product flowing again, so it wasn't until 2005 that management decided to let me incorporate all the fixes I thought were necessary to keep the power supplies running error free, and I was finally officially recognized for that.

Sometime in 2003. I was 43 years old now. Feather was a Quaker parrot that I took into my home. I got him from a female co-worker at General Dynamics. Feather would sleep with me every night—something that I still couldn't believe a bird would do, even after many years of experiencing this with Feather. I couldn't believe how loving birds could be. The affection and love and respect that Feather showed me, made me realize that all animals are sentient beings with feelings and personalities and a sense of morality, we just don't recognize it within them because we don't believe they can be that way and so we don't pay attention to them. They may not be as smart as us but that in no way denigrates them any more than a three-year-old toddler is any less human for being a three-year-old. Feather loved me more than anyone or anything I ever knew, and I loved Feather more than anyone or anything I ever knew. I cherished my time with Feather, and Feather was with me every single second of the day or night that I was home. She cuddled with me and even "purred" to show me that she loved me. I would whisper and blow into her ear and she would get goose bumps. Feather slept with me and ate with me and snuggled up against my hand whenever I was at my computer. I would give her kisses and then she would stare up at me and squint her eyes at me. Feather would nibble at the webbed part between my fingers, which was a very ticklish thing to do, so our relationship was give and take. I therefore learned the importance of give and take in relationships. I had wished that we would both live to a very old age together and then die together (or actually, I would die first and then Feather would die a few years later or so). But Feather died at eight years old on Nov 12th, 2010 at 3PM for unknown reasons and when she died, she took a little piece of my soul with her to his grave, as I, in turn, took a little piece of his soul with me to carry around forever.

In October of 2009 I went to Tibet with my wife and a Chinese tour group. We stopped at a hotel and the tour guide said don't go out and look at the military parade. I went out and looked. They stopped the parade and a General and an MP called me out to talk. I saluted the General and he asked why I saluted him. I told him he had this little plaque on his shirt that was full of awards and I said not just any man could earn those awards, and just by that alone he deserved more respect than other men that didn't have those awards. He asked if I was ever in the military and I said yes, the United States Marine Corps. He said weren't China and America enemies? I said how could I be enemies with the Chinese? I was in the middle of China with a Chinese tour group with my Chinese wife and her Chinese family and there were no other white people around for miles and miles. I said the only real enemies he was talking about were the politicians and congressmen always at each other's throats. He asked what I would do if I was still in the military and had to go to war against China. I said that was a very painful thing to ask me and I really didn't want to think about it. He asked why I was watching the parade and I said I didn't think it really mattered if I looked at it or not. For one thing, I had already seen the whole procession close up because our tour bus had passed them by on the way into town. There wasn't nothing I hadn't already seen before from a distance of about five feet, so if it really mattered, why did they allow us to view the procession on the way into town? He asked did they have these kinds of things in America. I said yes, but only if you lived close to a military base. He asked what it was like and I said that the Chinese version was better because they had more interesting things to look at. He said which was my favorite thing and I said the Humvee like truck with the multiple rocket launcher on top. He said didn't America have the same thing and I said yes, but it wasn't a very common sight. He said okay, told me to enjoy my stay, and left me alone.

It was at General Dynamics that I learned that I finally came to the realization that I had communication problems. This became most evident in my emails. People really didn't like the "tone of voice" of my emails, and for the life of me, I couldn't fix or correct or compensate for my alleged inability. I was constantly getting into trouble for my emails. Here I was, in my late forties, and I was being talked to like I was immature and childish and I thought, this wasn't right. I mean, I knew what they were complaining about was a legitimate complaint but (1) I was too old for anyone to have to talk to me about something as elementary as this, and (2) no matter how hard I tried, I couldn't fix this. I couldn't even pretend to fix it. There were other things that didn't add up and made me suspect I was autistic other than my emails, things like I had a very bad habit of drawing unwanted attention. I tried not to be the center of controversy but yet I usually stood right smack in the center of it. That's when I also started to notice that people reacted to things I said in unexpected ways. Sometimes I would inadvertently make people angry with me for no apparent logical reason. I talked to my then-supervisor about this. He said he had a grandson who was autistic and he suggested that maybe I was autistic too. I said I had heard that comment before but it wasn't acceptable because I was neither mentally retarded nor mute. He said that autism did not imply low IQ, that was just a stereotype, in fact, some autistic people had very high IQs, for example, those diagnosed with Asperger's. This eventually led me down the road to discover that I was autistic. Of course, the person I owe the most to in this regards is Stephanie Billman. Stephanie was the right person in the right place at the right time and I will never forget her.

The literature I found on autism was not very good or very thorough and it wasn't until I consulted a counselor, Stephanie Billman, on an unrelated issue, that I learned the true scope my condition. I was 51 years old at the time and with her guidance, she helped me explain so much to me about everything in my life that had no explanation before. Autism explained why people treated me the way they did at times. It explained all of my habits. I mean I never even thought about it before then, things like how I would spend anywhere from 60 to 80 hours a week, outside of work, rocking in my office chair while sitting at my computer and collecting hundreds of gigabytes of peer reviewed science journal articles. I loved doing this. I had absolutely no friends and I never even thought about it; I never felt lonely or that something might be wrong with me because I didn't have a single person I could truly call my friend. I was perfectly happy not having any friends. At first I thought about fixing

I imagine Stephanie Billman as the personification of Pandora. As the myth of Pandora has it, Pandora was the world's first woman, and she brought evil into the world by opening a jar filled with evil. I see variations of this myth, such as the myth of Adam and Eve. Why is it that women are portrayed as something that releases all manner of evil? If a woman dresses seductively and a man sees her and starts thinking sexually provocative thoughts, the man will not blame himself for having those thoughts, many men will blame the woman, as if she were to blame for his dirty thoughts instead of the thoughts being his own. That and the fact that women that are true to their nature, don't repress their emotions. They are experts on emotion and as part of their healing touch know how to instinctually release emotions in others.

Men repress their emotion as much as they can because they are fearful of them . . . and for good reason: emotions that are not dealt with properly can destroy you mentally. Men define themselves by what they can control and you can't control emotions, so that makes emotions "evil". So a man's solution is to repress and suppress as many emotions as they can. We are all going to Hell in a hand basket because men rule the world and they have emotionally sterilized the world so there is no life left in it.

Note that Pandora did not bring evil into the world, she only released it. As all the myths agree, it wasn't women that created evil or allowed evil to exist, it was a male or male God that did that. A man can't kill a Vietnamese soldier or an alleged Mideast terrorist by the thousands if he thinks of them as fellow human beings with families and feelings, with beautiful daughters and wives waiting for them at home. If you have feelings for them you wouldn't want to kill them, you would want to understand them. No one does "evil" things for no good reason or because they themselves are "pure evil".

All the terrible or uncomfortable thoughts and feelings I have had that Stephanie has brought out have been all my own. When I see evil or I see good in my memories or the world, it is only a reflection of what exists in my mind. If I can acknowledge and adjust for the evil that exists inside of me, my world becomes a place that no matter how bad other people are to me, it is still worth surviving for. It won't stop other people from trying to make evil real and try to force me to join in their delusions. They can still cause me pain or make me suffer, but they can never get me to accept their beliefs.

this, but then I realized what I really needed to do was stay true to myself and my true nature. I wouldn't have made it through life this far if I had tried to be someone else, someone else non-autistic.

Something that was very disconcerting at first was I discovered that most of my ideas and philosophies were not my own original ideas, but they were Autisms like: "I would rather be hurt by the truth than comforted by a lie" or I am good at computer programming or I love science and do well at it in school. Then there was the obsessions and stimming, yet none of these things are by freewill choice, instead they are the result of being autistic.

I have been to China with my wife about 10 times in 20 years. The purpose of our visit was always to see her family. Chinese are very family oriented—another reason why I originally wanted to marry a native Chinese woman. While I was there during my last visit, one of my relatives told me that I was going to White Cloud Mountains in the morning and I said, "No I wasn't. My wife and I had discussed this already and there was no point going there because the air was so hazy in Guangzhou that you couldn't see anything from that distance". So they suggested that this meant I didn't want to go and I had to tell her I didn't say that I liked or did not like to go to White Cloud Mountains, I only said that there was no point in going. So she suggested that this meant that I wanted to be away from my wife and do something else on my own and I had to tell her that, once again, I didn't say that I wanted to or did not want to do anything without my wife, I only said that going to the White Cloud Mountains was pointless since you couldn't see anything once you were there. This kind of nonsense banter went on for several minutes. I look forward to having only simple yes/no conversations so this kind of interaction is very unpleasant to me. Everything I discuss seems to be an argument and they seem to be twisting my words around instead of trying to understand what I am saying. I have had managers at work like this, people who want to constantly interrupt everything you say and put words in your mouth you never said or meant to imply. This is very dishonest behavior. My advice to Autistics is to avoid these people as much as possible but if you cannot avoid them, make sure that someone knows you are having a problem talking with these people. For my manager at work, I resort to Human Resources on a constant basis.

My niece-in-law is autistic. It took me awhile to figure this out. Well, I didn't suspect I was autistic until about 2009 and that's when

I started to suspect my niece was autistic too. At first I just thought she was just a little goofy, but as I learned over time what autism was, I also learned that she was definitely autistic as well. I regret not learning of this about her until after I applied for my wife's relatives to come over to America.

Now I can see in hindsight that I could have done much good in her life but because I didn't apply for her to come over to America, so I lost that opportunity. For example, she used to have an extreme reaction whenever someone went to touch her, for example, to hug her. One day I went to hug her and, as typical for her, she fell down to the ground. So I decided she wasn't going to do this to me anymore. I didn't know that either she or I was autistic, but I instinctively knew what to do . . . I fell down to the ground with her and joined her. So we were both lying there on the ground together and she is saying this is wrong of me to do this. I told her, yes it was wrong of me to do this and that people were staring at us and that this was uncomfortable for her but even more so for me her because I was an adult. She told me to get up and I said no. We were going to get up together or I wouldn't get up at. All I wanted to do was hug her, so if she agreed to do this together and let me hug her and see if she would like it or not, I wouldn't act like that, otherwise I would always act like that. So we got up together and we hugged. She had never hugged anyone of her own free will before, not even her mother, and she said it felt very comfortable. I told I her I know that it felt comfortable. And she never fell down on the ground anymore whenever someone went to hug her.

I asked my niece's mother what was wrong with her daughter. She said that her daughter fell out of her crib when she was a baby. I said did she see this for herself and she said yes. I told her she was full of it; she didn't see a damn thing, she was just repeating what other people told her she should be saying and not something she saw for herself. I told her that if she researched the literature she would see that brain damage never causes symptoms like her daughter had. No one has ever become autistic from having an automobile accident. No adult has ever fallen down, hit their head, and become autistic. So how could it ever possibly be common only for children below the age of three to have "brain damage" that causes autism?

Appendix A

WHAT EXACTLY IS AUTISM?

Autism is clearly and officially defined by the APA DSM-5 (American Psychiatric Association Diagnostic and Statistical Manual of Mental Disorders—Revision Five). To be classified as autistic, you must be considered socially abnormal, demonstrate poor use of body language, and be capable of mainly having only superficial relationships with your peers. You must have two out of four of the following behaviors:

1. Repetitive mannerisms, like echolalia, pacing, or are too fidgety ("stimming"),
2. Strict adherence (or attach too much importance) to routine(s),
3. Intense but limited and unusual interests, or
4. Over- or insensitivity to sensory stimulus.

All of these symptoms must have been present in early childhood and they must impair or limit the person's ability to function in society. Note that it doesn't say an autistic person can't function in society, only that they are impaired or limited in that ability. Note that disability does not mean inability. Finally note that it does not state that there are any such things as "classical autism", "Aspergers", or "high-functioning autism"—you are either autistic or you are not autistic. There is no such thing as "autistic-like" or anything in-between autistic and non-autistic. The only thing that does matter when describing autism are degrees of autism: level one, two, or three, with level three being completely unable to function and level one being the equivalent of what people call "high functioning". Yet "high functioning" doesn't mean a thing when you are still "impaired", so what does the term "high functioning" actually mean? In psychology, "high functioning" means to have an IQ above 70, but IQ is irrelevant to whether one has autism or not. When most people talk about high functioning, they are talking about the ability to function alone in life. Functioning in life consists of many things, the least of which consists of:

1. Being independent
2. Being responsible
3. Finding a job
4. Keeping a job
5. Finding a place to live
6. Finding a way to get around (transportation)

How many of us are able to fully function in life without ANY outside help whatsoever? What if you were to suddenly become stranded in the middle of a rain forest? How well would you survive on your own then? Keep this in mind before judging the ability of those with autism to survive on their own or not, since functioning is a matter of degrees and not absolutes. So on a deeper level, when we speak of functioning in respect to autism, we are mainly referring to social functioning, which consists of:

1. Getting along with others
2. Avoiding unnecessary conflict
3. Reasonable and prudent use of aggression
4. Appropriate use of humor
5. Maintaining proper grooming habits
6. Maintaining diplomacy
7. Being polite

Yet the inability to conform to a particular society's ideals of what each of these items means makes a person "abnormal" in their eyes, whether they are high-functioning or not. Of course, that requires us to define what "normal" is and therein lays the problem because if normal means what most people do or say, then warmongering, delusions of things that only exist in their imaginations (communist threat, ghosts, ESP, the supernatural, vampires), high divorce rates, primitive and superstitious thinking, toleration of intolerance, and illogical thinking, are all "normal" then . . .

> *"Look at all the incredible savagery going on in our so-called civilized world: it all comes from human beings and the spiritual condition they are in! Look at the devilish engines of destruction! They are invented by completely innocuous gentlemen, reasonable, respectable citizens who are everything we could wish to be. And when the whole thing blows up and an indescribable hell of destruction is let loose, nobody seems to be responsible. It simply happens, and yet it is all man-made. But since everybody is blindly convinced that he is nothing more than his own extremely unassuming and insignificant conscious self, which performs its duties decently and earns a moderate living, nobody is aware that this whole rationalistically organized conglomeration we call a 'state' or a 'nation' is driven on by a seemingly impersonal, invisible but terrifying power which nobody and nothing can check. This ghastly power is mostly explained as fear of the neighboring nation, which is supposed to be possessed by a malevolent fiend. Since nobody is capable of recognizing just where and how much he himself is possessed and unconscious, he simply projects his own condition upon his neighbor, and thus it becomes a sacred duty to have the biggest guns and the most poisonous gas. The worst of it is that he is quite right. All one's neighbours are in the grip of some uncontrolled and uncontrollable fear, just like oneself. In lunatic asylums it is a well-known fact that patients are far more dangerous when suffering from fear than when moved by rage or hatred"*—Jung, C.G. (1953) TWO ESSAYS ON ANALYTICAL PSYCHOLOGY, The Collected Works of C.G. Jung (Vol 11 para 85) R.F. Hull (Editor/Translator) published 1969

> *". . . every man is, in a certain sense, unconsciously a worse man when he is in society than when acting alone;*

for he is carried by society and to that extent relieved of his individual responsibility. ANY large company composed of wholly admirable persons has the morality and intelligence of an unwieldy, stupid, and violent animal. The bigger the organization, the more unavoidable is its immorality and blind stupidity . . . Society, by automatically stressing all the collective qualities in its individual representatives, puts a premium on mediocrity, on everything that settles down to vegetate in an easy, irresponsible way. Individuality will eventually be driven to the wall . . . without freedom there can be no morality"—Jung, C.G. (1958) TWO ESSAYS ON ANALYTICAL PSYCHOLOGY, The Collected Works of C.G. Jung (Vol 7 para 240) R.F. Hull (Editor/Translator) published 1969

. . . why would anyone in their right mind, want to be normal?

I like the term "typical" instead of "normal" though because it tells it like it is: Autistics aren't abnormal but rather are atypical. The rest of you are not normal, but rather are NTs (read: neurobiologically typical or neurotypical), and being typical does not mean that any, much less all of you, are paragons of mental health, you are only typical representations of what being human is like. This raises the possibility of imagining what if Autistics were the majority instead of the minority—the tables would be turned! What we call NT today instead would be classified as pathological and it would be the Autistics that were NT. Imagine how the Autistic Psychiatric Association's Diagnostic and Statistical Manual of Mental Disorders would describe NTs then . . .

"Neurotypical syndrome is a neurobiological disorder characterized by preoccupation with social concerns, delusions of superiority, and obsession with conformity. Neurotypical individuals often assume that their experience of the world is either the only one, or the only correct one. NTs find it difficult to be alone. NTs are often intolerant of seemingly minor differences in others. When in groups NTs are socially and behaviorally rigid, and frequently insist upon the performance of dysfunctional, destructive, and even impossible rituals as

a way of maintaining group identity. NTs find it difficult to communicate directly, and have a much higher incidence of lying as compared to persons on the autistic spectrum. NT is believed to be genetic in origin. Autopsies have shown the brain of the neurotypical is typically smaller than that of an autistic individual and may have overdeveloped areas related to social behavior."—Muskie (1999) INSTITUTE FOR THE STUDY OF THE NEUROLOGICALLY TYPICAL. Retrieved February 10th, 2013 from http://isnt.autistics. org/isnt text.html.

You naturally expect Autistics to react certain ways to things you say or do, and when that doesn't happen you will judge that person to be irritating and offensive, but it certainly won't be because they are irritating or offensive. While, "[The human brain seems to] *be genetically programmed to trigger consistently similar mental reproductions of similar events in the external world, plus consistently similar emotional and physical responses to those reproductions*" (Bower, T (1971, Oct). THE OBJECT IN THE WORLD OF THE INFANT, Sci American, pg 30-38), clearly Autistics are not programmed to be the same as everyone else; they have very different ideas and thoughts and therefore very different emotional and physical responses to those mental reproductions that those different ideas and thoughts cause. Being different is what makes Autistics "rub people the wrong way".

Therefore if you want to have a serious heart-to-heart talk with an Autistic, take the advice of an Autistic and learn to follow these simple rules of engagement:

1.   Never be rhetorical
2.   Never be sarcastic
3.   Don't joke around
4.   Don't use analogies
5.   Don't have a hidden agenda
6.   Avoid using slang
7.   Remember that no subject or topic is taboo to an Autistic
8.   Facts are never good or bad or something to take personally, they are just data points
9.   Never dismiss anything they tell you as trivial or unimportant

10. Never assume they have a hidden agenda
11. If you are angry or annoyed, do not look at them while talking
12. If you are confused or concerned, do not look at them while talking
13. Try to be very, very precise in your terminology
14. Always be honest to the extreme
15. When listening, never try to "read between the lines" with anything they say
16. Be consistent in your thinking style
17. Be transparent, i.e.—have nothing to hide
18. Listen very, very carefully to any replies
19. Take everything they say, literally
20. If you don't want to know the truth about yourself, don't ask an autistic person
21. Try not to be offended by anything they say

From childhood to adulthood, what would you do and how would you feel if, with very rare exceptions, everyone you came across rejected you as you are, and then these same people would try to force their way of thinking, their way of relating, upon you? When I say "everyone", I mean everyone: your mom, your dad, your sister, your brother, your relatives, and so on. No matter what you did or said, whether it be your pacing or rocking or stimming, people wouldn't like it—there would be no pleasing them. I tell you what you would feel, you would feel stressed out and you would have all the health problems that come with being stressed out. Maybe you would have Irritable Bowel Syndrome or have an over-active immune system or lose your appetite and be a picky eater. And I tell you what you would do, you would withdraw and isolate yourself from everyone that you could. You would feel and act anxious, not knowing what innocent little thing you did or said would pop up in a conversation so that people could denounce you for "acting up again".

Autistics shouldn't have to become drug-induced zombies so as to not attract any attention by having us quietly stay out of your way. I would like to see you start encouraging behaviors and accepting behaviors, not the other way around. Yes, many of our behaviors and ways of thinking/perceiving may seem very strange to you, but they harm no one, so learn to live with them, just as we have learned to live with yours.

I don't know if autistic brains are wired differently than non-autistic brains, but I do know non-Autistics see things differently than Autistics do and Autistics see things differently than non-Autistics do. Unfortunately, one of the many ways Autistics see the world differently from non-Autistics is determined by their permanently immature and naïve-like nature. It makes them naturally vulnerable or "easy prey". This is something that cannot be fixed or masked. You cannot ask a three-year old to act like a 23-year old because they have no idea what that means. There is only one way for a person to act like they are 23-years old and that is for them to actually be 23-years old (or older). Sure they can put on an act, if they have been prompted on what to do or say, but if what they encounter is something outside of the scripting they have been prompted to imitate, it will appear out-of-place. Like the three-year old trying to act like a 23-year old, Autistics know they don't fit in socially but they also know they can never do anything to make themselves fit in either. Some Autistics make grand attempts to appear like they fit in but every single one of them will still ultimately fail in the end. This is the world that Autistics live in.

At the time of this writing I was 50-something years old, so clearly Autism is not something you will outgrow. If it were something that could be outgrown, where are all the ex-autistic people then?

Note that autism isn't necessarily congenital. Being mentally retarded can cause autism. So can being institutionalized, in fact, institutionalized caused autism is indistinguishable from congenital autism.

Having a familiar routine helps establish normalcy in an uncertain world, therefore I believe that the obsession with routines is not a primary trait for Autistics but it is only a pacifier for deeper issues not yet resolved. The more routines that make one feel normal, the more tolerable the un-normal events will be.

Appendix B

SURVIVING AUTISM

DESPITE BEING AUTISTIC, I had worked at EF Data for 13 years and at General Dynamics for 10. I had been married since 1991 and had paid off my home in 2007. I currently own two Lexus (one has been paid off; the other has not) and my biggest worry until that time was about how, and if, I was ever going to retire. Some people would say that makes me a successful person. I'm not interested in labels like that but I sometimes wonder that if I had known I was autistic when I was younger, would I have still become the "successful" person I am today? Nobody ever told me that something as simple as driving a car or managing a budget or having a steady job or having a long term relationship were individually very rare but nearly almost impossible to have all of them at the same when you are autistic. Surviving the orphanage, the bullying, the attempted murders, and teaching myself Cantonese was not supposed to be an easy thing to learn either. I wish someone had been kind enough to interrupt me while I was doing these "impossible" things so I could have saved myself a lot of time and trouble by failing to do them like I was supposed to.

It was Stephanie Billman, my friend and psychotherapist, who first told me that I was unique because I was autistic and "successful". She told me that I could help other Autistics and their significant others that worried about them, if I would only publish a book about my life experiences. She encouraged me to participate in the autism community—online and locally, although I failed with the online part. I went to The Melmed Center in Scottsdale, Arizona and got an official diagnosis for my autism, just like she told me to do. I trusted her and thought I was doing something good.

But I did something stupid on my own in the meantime. I had been so successful at surviving autism that I forgot all the hard work and painful lessons I learned to become successful. I was tired of pretending to not exist, by being withdrawn, although I enjoyed the peace and quiet that being very withdrawn brought me. I just wanted to be true to myself and act and dress and talk the way I naturally wanted to act, dress, and talk. So I quickly dropped 60 pounds and went from a 46 inch waist to a 36 inch waist. I got my ears pierced and started wearing a Fedora. I wore clothes that were mismatched in color, but they were nice, bright colors that I liked. Wherever I went, whether at work or at the mall, I would carry my portable MP3 player and I would "stim to beat" in public, for all to see—not that I wanted attention, but because I enjoyed doing it for myself. Of course I still hated getting attention, but I tolerated it because I believed Stephanie Billman when she told me that someday I would be famous, so I thought I might as well try to get used to having attention. When people talked nasty to me at work, I would talk nasty right back to them. People freaked out. Even my wife couldn't handle it. Some people tried force me or talk me into changing back. I thought that if they couldn't handle my change that this was their problem, not mine, so I ignored them.

=== It was a complete and total disaster ===

I got called into HR (Human Resources) at General Dynamics about ten times after I stopped being as withdrawn as I used to be. My workplace was intolerant of my "stimming to the beat" because it was "too distracting". Everyone started blaming my behavioral changes at work on a black woman I hung out with at lunch and break. I got into trouble for cussing at a janitor who called me ugly. To get people to stop talking nasty to me, I went to HR and told them what they were saying to me. I told HR that I was autistic and therefore vulnerable and an easy target for bullying; that I just wanted to be myself and be left alone, but going to HR just made people even more angry with me. I can easily relate to the Autistic who said, "There is something wrong with me. I can't do things right. Everyone is mad at me. No matter how hard I try, something goes wrong. Other people can do the things I can't. It must be my fault that I'm having so much trouble"—Spicer, David (1998) SELF-AWARENESS IN LIVING WITH ASPERGER SYNDROME. Retrieved February 10th, 2013 from http://bellsouthpwp.net/d/s/dspicer/aware.html.

Finally one day, I got into a lot of trouble for something truly bad I did. I then decided that I was going to use this incident as a way to prove that I was vulnerable and needed sheltering from the bullying I was receiving. I told HR that if I wasn't autistic, I would have never been called in for any violation because the same people that turned me in for a violation were themselves, either violating a serious rule themselves or were turning a deaf eye to other people that were committing serious violations. Because I claimed I was autistic, I was forced to file a request for a disability accommodation. I was also forced to get The Melmed Center to fill out a form for Occupational HR so that I could be relocated to a job more suitable for a person with autism. I didn't cherish the thought of being forced to do these things and being told what I could and couldn't do. Just because I didn't like or fit into a production environment doesn't mean I wanted to work somewhere else. I was making it work, even though I was miserable doing it. I mean, I had been at GD for ten years and no one ever noticed I was autistic or ever had an issue or complaint against me (well . . . for the most part that is), and now I had to turn my life upside-down because I was labeled "autistic"?

I was learning that, once again, autism brings out best and the worst in people. I had people that either really hated me or really liked me—with nothing inbetween—I already knew that was just the way life is but the thing is, people feel compelled to come out and tell you or show you that they hate you when you are autistic and not withdrawn. They can't just leave you alone. It is like going into a shoe store to stare at shoes you don't like. Why would you do that? People were unfairly judgemental of me but I also learned a lesson. I grew up to be successful because I was left alone to devise my own plans and schemes without assitance or sheltering.

What scheme did I use to survive by? First and foremost, I minimized my interactions with people, i.e.—I was very withdrawn. I would avoid any and all interaction with people that I could at work, even the most simple of interactions like "Hello" or "Good morning". My advice is, if you are autistic that is, you don't want to draw any attention to yourself whatsoever. When you dress, dress to be boring.

Wear plain clothes in very drab neutral colors, like gray or black or denim blue. Let people believe that you are very shy—because they will believe that—and in my case, I could add that I was an orphan and then they would act like that explained why I was so unsocial. Never brag about anything you have ever done or do. If people say bad things to you, which they often do, don't say anything at all in response, in the future just avoid them at all costs and they will think you are antisocial and hate you for it, but it is better for them to think you are antisocial and hate you then to respond to them and allow other people to see you are different or get yourself in trouble with Human Resources.

So getting back to the original topic, how did I become "successful" at being married for over 20 years? Well it certainly wasn't because I minimized my interactions like I did at work, although I did do that to some degree. No, what I had to do was learn to give dignity and to earn respect from my partner. How does one earn respect in a relationship? By being ever willing to make sacrifices. By making sacrifices, which can be in the form of money or time or not complaining when I am obviously upset, I am demonstrating to my partner how much I value them. How does one give someone else dignity? By being forgiving and tolerant of your partners many faults and idiosyncrasies. If you overlook the faults of your partner, they will be more willing to overlook yours. And I listen and respond to my partner's needs so if my partner wants to be held or touched (in a sexual or non-sexual way), I give it to them—or if they don't want to be touched or held, I avoid doing so.

A Chinese woman asked me a question the other day, after all the Hell I went through growing up, how did I find the will to live; what gave me meaning in my life. Was it a belief in God? You know what I said to her? What gave me the will to live wasn't a belief in a make believe God that you cannot hear, see, smell, taste, or feel. No, it was in real life women that you can hear, see, smell, taste, and feel. And what I felt was nurturing, affectionate, accepting, and understanding. Only women have the healing touch, although not every woman has it, and as an Autistic, I had lots of times I needed a healing touch.

Appendix C

KARMA AND DHARMA

I HAVE SPENT MANY years in China and have objectively observed many things about the Chinese person, including their religions and philosophies. One of the things that caught my attention was their concept of karma, so let's talk about karma.

Karma had been translated as "action", but people in general misinterpret this to mean "every action has a reaction". They believe that the reactions are immediate and are simply just a variation of the barbaric and unjust concept of the "eye for an eye, tooth for a tooth" philosophy. Yet others believe karma as something one can also accumulate, like money in a bank account. All of this is inaccurate. Let me correct this by giving you some examples . . .

. . . A person can cause another person to die because their intentions were hateful or because their intentions were self-defense or because it was an accident. These are three completely different intentions yet they all result in the same consequence. It would not make sense that the karma in all three cases would be exactly the same. No, karma is about intentions and merit is the value of your intentions. You can be a person full of good intentions or a person full of bad intentions and it is the value of those intentions that earn you the right to have a better future life or a worse future life.

. . . A man is going out for a drive in the country. He turns a blind corner and finds that a bridge is out and turns around. He was lucky he wasn't speeding or he would have gone over the edge. A quarter-of-a-mile down the road from the bridge is a rest stop and he pulls over. He overhears a group of kids talking about having a race over the path that the out-of-order bridge is on. The man has an opportunity to warn them but takes no action. The kids die. Now the question is, how will this man's karma change his merit? Since he committed no action, can he have accumulated good or bad merit? In this case, the man who saw an opportunity to prevent something awful from happening but allowed it to happen anyways, has accumulated a psychological debt, a bad merit.

. . . I noticed while growing up in the '60s how Americans made fun of fat people. It was everywhere: on TV, at school, at home, in the jokes people told. One of the more popular taunts from that era that I remember about being fat was, "Fatty, fatty, two-by-four, can't fit through the kitchen door", among other derogatory things. Yet now, less than fifty years later, no one dares make those kinds of taunts anymore because it would be a case of the pot calling the kettle black. Americans have grown up to become the very thing they despised in the 60's—big, fat, two-by-fours. This last example is a very good example for you of the concept of karma:

1. The people's intention was to humiliate and insult those more unfortunate then themselves—calling the few fat children in their school, "big, fat two-by-fours".
2. Those intentions activated their karma and the result of their karma was to accumulate bad merit.
3. The bad merit made it possible for them to "pay the entrance fee" to a world or way of living that reflected what they deserved—being big, fat two-by-fours.

These "ways of living", or "worlds" as Siddhartha put it, are part of an endless insufferable circle of life called dharma. They are the many fates waiting to be reaped by you for all the karma you have sown. The logic is simple—if it is okay to humiliate and insult others when they are down then it is okay for others to humiliate and insult you when you are down. For better or worse, we get what we know we deserve. It is an inexorable psychological law. It all makes me wonder what karma will bring to Americans for all those dumb blonde girl jokes they used to tell?

Siddhartha said we can never eliminate suffering. To live is to suffer and that is what dharma is all about. This makes it sound like life is about nothing but suffering but all it really means is that everyone has to suffer at least once during their lifetime. Death of yourself or a loved one is a form of suffering. People can also suffer from many of life's common problems but the amount of suffering they can cause is all relative—what is a major problem to one person can be minor to another and vice versa. Some Buddhists even go so far as to say that "everyone has exactly 82 problems". So if you are a living being, you can be guaranteed that you will suffer.

I have always suffered. I am still suffering. But I've seen what Siddhartha wrote. And I've seen the truth in what Siddhartha said. He knew suffering. I can see and feel it in what he said. And I know that suffering is what my life is all about. It's my fate, bought and paid for by my merits, which I accumulated in some past life or lives by my demonstrated intentions, and nothing can undo that. Do you know what it feels like for people to despise you, even when you mean no harm but only good? I know what it's like to suffer very greatly. As a child I had other children try to take my life. I had adults do the same. I've been humiliated and intimidated and insulted. I've been bullied by girls and boys and adults. But you know what? I'm still here.

I think about all that hate. There are so many people that love to hate. I can taste their hate. And I wonder why they love it so much because it is so bitter. But what little love there is in the world has made it all bearable. Even if I never find true love, it gives me hope to imagine that I can. That's why I'm still here. I'm not parroting some belief or philosophy or religious text, I'm speaking from my heart. I know what suffering is and I know what love is. I don't have faith in words. I have faith in facts and logic—and the feelings that arise from knowing those facts and logic. Notice how I say "I'm still here" but I don't say "I'm still standing". That's because I'm not still standing.

Like Humpty Dumpty, the pieces of my life can never be put together again.

So karma is more than just a word all by itself, it is a concept behind a whole theory. It should be obvious by now that every action does indeed have a consequence, but now we also can understand that even every non-action also has a consequence. From a psychological point-of-view, it is the intentions of the person that what matters most, and not the actions or the consequences, and together they develop a person's merit, which in turn helps determine a person's future fate. Merit is something that one can only accumulate. Karma isn't just about visible actions or visible consequences, it is about invisible intentions.

Yet there is more. They say the path to Hell is lined with good intentions and this is true. If you mean something for good and it causes harm, you know you shouldn't be doing it. Something is wrong with your philosophy or logic if your intentions are good but it results in harm.

In Buddhism the question comes up often about who am I and what am I? This seems like a silly question on a superficial level but on a deeper level it is very profound. I am autistic but exactly what does that mean? Is autism the "real me"? If not, who am "I" and what am I really like on the inside? If I was not autistic, would the real "me" cease to exist? If I was not autistic, would I still be me or would I be someone else?

Autistics are not normal people trapped inside a damaged shell. Autism is an inseparable part of an Autistics being. If you want to help autistic people, stop trying to shoehorn them into your tiny little world. Society needs to adapt itself to autism more so than the other way around. All I ever hear from people is how Autistics need to change their "bad" behaviors (a few of which truly are bad and should be changed) yet I don't very often hear people encouraging their very many harmless behaviors. Instead, it seems to me like nothing Autistics ever do is acceptable to the typical person and these people will only be satisfied if Autistics modify their behaviors so that they can act just like them. I want you to think about this and change your approach to be more accepting, understanding, and affectionate instead of the current thoughtless harmful things I read about people performing on Autistics such as:

- Electroshock "therapy"
- Indiscriminate use of prescription drugs (chemical restraint)
- Industrial strength bleach enemas

The Buddhist version of Hell predates the Christian one by over a thousand years and it is not a place of eternal torture. In Buddhism, Hell is a lesson. Yet many people blindly believe in a God, a God that would randomly put me on Earth to suffer so much for no good reason, while others would live a life of luxury. Then, in the end, the vast majority of people would all go to the same place forever and ever, another place of great suffering, Hell. Yet the path to Heaven is a tiny little off-beaten trail that even if you do manage to find it, it dead ends with a narrow locked gate, with limited admission. This has to make you wonder that if this was that version of God's Universe, and He could do whatever He wants with it, why would He allow Hell to remain open instead of closing down the gates to Hell thousands of years ago, that way only a few thousand people would go there instead of the current billions and billions—wouldn't that have been the more "loving-kind" thing to do? Doesn't God believe in damage control?

After I had found out I was autistic, I followed Stephanie Billman's advice and tried to get involved with the autistic community, mainly by volunteering or going to group meetings. Yet no matter what I did, nothing worked out. Everything was thwarted or ignored or rejected or uneventful. Even the biography I tried to write was undermined—the Cold Cases Division at the Sheriff's Department in Los Angeles said that even though I gave them real names, locations, and approximate dates, it still wasn't enough information to track down the murders I reported to them that happened 40 years ago, despite having read accounts on the Internet and newspapers about cold cases being solved with much less information than I have given them, murders that had taken place 46 years ago or more. I wanted to accumulate good merit by doing good things but my every effort is thwarted in one way or another. If I'm being thwarted over this because of past bad merit, it wouldn't make sense because it would be inconsiderate and uncompassionate to not be able to do what I am attempting to do for people. Then I thought about it. Maybe it's because of their bad merit, not mine, that I'm being thwarted from being able to help them. Maybe it would be like the New Age rumor that the gas crisis would have never happened or we could have been colonizing space by now, if the Holocaust had not happened; that the one person who could have saved us from the gas crisis by inventing anti-gravity or some other such thing, was murdered, and no one stepped up in time to stop it from happening. We just let it happen because it wasn't our business or concern.

But somebody out there deserves my help, don't they?

Appendix D

BULLYING AND VIOLENCE

As you can tell from my autobiography, I was very much bullied as a child, not only just by boys my own age, but by girls and adults of all ages. The epitome of this bullying occurred while I was at the Hippos foster home, therefore I am quite familiar with the phenomenon of bullying. So let me educate you on what bullies and bullying is really all about instead of the nonsense that is being spread about in the media today . . .

The typical bully has been described as an unhappy, overactive, underachiever who feels powerless and without any control over their personal lives. These are the very rare type people which get temporary pleasure from having complete control over others while giving them pain, yet these kinds of bullies are the most stereotyped because they are the most visible. It's just like the fact that the typical gay person doesn't act gay at all. It's the very rare but flamboyant gays that are most visible and become the stereotype, so you never really learn what a typical gay person acts like due to this stereotyping. The reality is, the best and most common bullies are upstanding people in their communities. In my case they were the jocks at Giano or one of my many foster parents. Bullying isn't always just about picking on you or violence either. Real life bullies will most likely desire something unusual from you like unrestrained sex, high respect, adoration, indulgence in some perversion, etc.

Bullies will not pick on you unless they know you can do absolutely nothing about it in return. Experienced bullies know exactly what it will take to hurt you physically and/or emotionally. A bully will only attack those weaker than themselves so they know they have nothing to fear from you . . . ever. Bullies are not cowards or people with low self-esteem or people insecure about themselves. That is an ignorant lie.

Many bullies start out by "testing the waters"—seeing how you react to small things. If they like what they see, they escalate. Authorities have to be willing to intervene, even for small things. My experience is that most authorities don't give a shit. That's why you can have children that are constantly bullied, put into hospitals or killed, and authorities claim ignorance or feign concern in hindsight, but in reality they never really tried to do anything about it or even paid attention to it to begin with. They have more "important things" to do, like collecting their paychecks.

I have heard some people claim that when confronted by bullies, to "stand your ground so the bullies will back down". I have heard other people claim that all you need to do is just "walk away and hold your head high". This is the kind of advice that will get you killed by real life bullies. Their advice also reflects the silly American myth of the one-man hero; that all you have to do is transform yourself into the superman you were always meant to be and your enemies will "scatter like the cowards they really are". Bullies want to intimidate, embarrass, humiliate, or all the above so even if you could walk away or they would allow you to walk away for no reason, and you decided to hold your head held high to show them they had no effect on you, they would know they failed to bully you and now they will try even harder the next time—and there definitely will be a next time.

Personally, I find overreacting works best when dealing with teasing or bullying. If I can't tell someone is picking on me or bullying me, better safe than sorry. As a vulnerable working adult, I often go to Human Resources (when I'm not being withdrawn, of course). Unfortunately Human Resources might find me annoying or immature and the person reported on might be truly offended if no harm to me was intended, but that is the chance I feel I have to take. Bullies will play games and pretend to be offended if you report them, then they will try to "win" you back into their confidence where they can turn on you and make you suffer even more.

Sometimes you have to accept the fact that you will be bullied and there is absolutely nothing you can do about it except to try and minimize the damage.

Note that being picked on and being bullied are not the same thing. People confuse the two. I've seen friends pick on each other, but friends never bully each other. Where do you draw the line? Sometimes there are gray areas. If a person is oversensitive—and Autistic people tend to be oversensitive—they can perceive anything and everything as being picked on or bullied. For an Autistic, determining if a comment is "harmless" or when it is meant to be hurtful, can be very difficult sometimes. And if you can't tell if a comment was meant to be hurtful at first, by the time you do figure it out, it will have escalated into bullying—but by then it is too late, a precedence has been set.

Friends hit each other and adults will call it "being playful". But if you don't know how to play that game, what can start out as playful can turn into a fistfight. For an Autistic, aggression is extremely difficult to deal with. I still can't deal with it, even after 50 years. But you can't always avoid doing anything when confronted with aggression. Sometimes your life can be at stake, as was mine many times. As an Autistic, you are always wondering if you are overreacting or if you did the right thing. It is frustrating and scary. Communication between parents and child is very, very, very important when it comes to bullying. An autistic child has to know they can constantly and annoyingly come to you to ask questions about whether a comment was meant to be playful or hurtful.

Even autistic people can be bullies, as I discovered on Twitter one day when I innocently asked an autistic woman to refrain from saying degrading things about herself, and she proceeded to attack me, calling me a "Nazi" and other unprovoked derogatory names. That is a mild case and it isn't the only time Autistics have been known to be bullies . . .

> *"Recently we have witnessed the phenomenon of 'autistic bullies'*
> *(for the lack of a better term). These are newly diagnosed*
> *individuals who suddenly discover that all their past problems*
> *can be explained by somebody else's fault. They do not seek*
> *the understanding of what is different about them and how*

they can compensate their weaknesses and use these differences for their advantage, but rather blame NTs [non-Autistics] (both parents and professionals) for all their misfortune. The fact is, these individuals, being unaware of their condition in the past, have developed a very low self-esteem. The diagnosis for them has provided the explanations of others' fault in all their past and present problems. Because of their (negative) experiences they still operate with the concepts they used in the past when being bullied. Whatever is said to them (even if you agree with some of their views but use different words), they would misinterpret and twist the message. And don't you dare to correct them! ('Sorry, you have misunderstood me') If you do you may find yourself on the receiving end of their rage—'He/ she called me an idiot, stupid and cognitively ill!' Rather than understanding and addressing their difficulties, they criticize everything and everybody.

After many years of having been bullied, they become bullies themselves. As a young AS lady put it—'sometimes former victims make the most efficient perpetuators'. They may bully and insult others in order to compensate for their low self-esteem. They project their own failings and insecurities on other people, and attack and criticize in others the very problems they themselves experience. And it is not only the parents and professionals who would be hurt by their attacks. Other autistic individuals, who have different views and are prepared to address their difficulties, become perfect targets for these autistic bullies. Those who cooperate with parents and professionals are labeled 'token autistics'. This is very unfortunate, because very few individuals may alienate others (who accept and appreciate their autism but do not idealize it) from advocacy for the understanding and acceptance of differences. This 'aggressive advocacy' is more of a hindrance than promotion of acceptance. It is not surprising, therefore, that many HF and AS people want nothing to do with this sort of advocacy. They find the tactics 'autistic bullies' use questionable at best, because they try to advocate in the midst of hatred for others, and for people claiming to fight for the rights of others it is both demoralizing and frightening (Smith 2005). In his article 'Why I don't want to be an autistic advocate anymore' (2005), Joel Smith enumerates several reasons why negative traits brought into the autistic advocacy community by a few individuals, in fact, interferes with true advocacy.

- *Too many who claim to be autistic advocates believe the autistics should get rights because they have intelligence that the rests of the world lacks.*
- *Too many who claim to be autistic advocates believe that their subgroup of autistics is more able to be the voice of autism than other subgroups*
- *Too many who claim to be autistic advocates look at themselves and their own personal needs above all other autistics*
- *Those who shout about how horrible those awful NTs are, are themselves engaged in exactly the same negative acts they accuse NTs of doing, e.g.—bullying, favouritism, hero-worship*

The author concludes that maybe when autistic communities figure out a way to represent the cause without fighting each other, and without trying to exalt themselves above other groups of non-autistics, then it will be worthwhile to promote a true advocacy for the rights of all people, including autistics (Smith 2005)"—Bogdashina, Olga (2006). THEORY OF MIND AND THE TRIAD OF PERSPECTIVES ON AUTISM AND ASPERGER SYNDROME: A VIEW FROM THE BRIDGE [Kindle Edition], pgs 169-171. Author Smith, J (2005) cited by Bogdashina (2006) refers to WHY I DON'T WANT TO BE AN AUTISTIC ADVOCATE ANYMORE from www.autistics.org/library/ noautadvocate.html.

I often say the biggest problem with bullying isn't with the bullying itself, but with the parents not listening to the bullied child's screams for help. I had scary-looking temper tantrums while I was at the Gestalt's, but if only the adults had listened to me and either removed me from that detrimental environment or disciplined the other kids instead of me, I would have had no temper tantrums. A bullied child learns to either give up hope or they learn to become violent themselves.

Since I brought up the topic of violence, let's take a moment and talk about violence and autism. What does it take to be a serial killer and how does that compare to being autistic? Read http://www.trutv. com/library/crime/serial_killers/notorious/tick/victims_1.html, then ask yourself how many traits do Autistics have in common with serial killers as described in that article? In general, none, but I scored four out of five but I will never become a serial killer. How so? Because I'm autistic. No serial killer has ever been autistic.

Now let's talk about what it takes to be a terrorist. See http:// dspace.mit.edu/openaccess-disseminate/1721.1/57901. See anything in that article that talks about autism? Nope. The qualities required are the opposite of autism.

Gavin De Becker has a book entitled KEEPING CHILDREN & TEENAGERS SAFE. Now I respect Gavin and his advice for the most part. He has been an advisor to Presidents so I respect his experience. So what does Gavin say about Autistics in his book I mentioned above? He says autistic children should not live in a household that has guns or hunts. He seems to be saying that Autistics can't be trusted with guns because Autistics are an inherent danger to society, merely because they're autistic.

James Eagan Holmes went on a rampage at a theater in Aurora, Colorado on July of 2012, killing 12 and injuring 58 people. Joe Scarborough of MSNBC went on to claim that, "You have these people that are somewhere . . . on the autism scale . . . it happens more often than not . . . we see too many shooters in these types of tragedies bearing the same characteristics mentally".

I've always said that autism brings out the worst and the best in people. So these are all examples of what is the worst in people: Blatant lies and cruel accusations. People will believe all this nonsense about Autistics being violence prone or serial killers or terrorists because Autistics are known for having scary temper tantrums. The comments made by Gavin De Becker and Joe Scarborough aren't backed up by facts or statistics. Autistics are no more or no less prone to deadly violence than the rest of the general population. To paint a broad brush and say that by nature Autistics are inherently dangerous to society is profiling in the worst way.

There may be one exception in all of human history to this rule: Adam Lanza, so let's talk about Adam Lanza. You can't blame a mass murder on a man just because he was autistic. Was it autism that was behind the Columbine massacre or the Virginia Tech shootings or the Success Tech shootings or the Northern Illinois University shootings or the Bridgeville, Pennsylvania LA Fitness shootings or the San Mateo High School shootings or the Chardon High School shootings? Absolutely not, but I still wondered what do all the shooters behind these incidents have in common? I know what they have in common, they were all described as bullied or outcast. That's strange, because Autistics are very much bullied and outcasts, so you might think that they therefore would be much more prone to being shooters, yet in all of history, only one Autistic has ever done so. Why is that? I will tell you why, because I know what was going through Adam Lanza's mind when he set out to kill all those people, and so do you. You see, Adam Lanza was your own personal creation. He was your dream come true—which only reinforces the adage to be careful for what you wish for because you just might get your wish come true. It also makes him your karma. Let me explain . . .

Society demonstrates what it values most by how much money it pours into a cause or person. You are the ones that pay Hollywood lots of money to show you generous amounts of movies and TV shows that glorify guns and death. All your superheroes have awesome looking guns at their disposal. And when your Hollywood heroes can't reason with their enemies, they go after them with their awesome looking guns blazing. Rambo. John Wayne. James Bond. Terminator. Neo. Transformers. Avatar. You pay lots of money for games where you can pretend to murder and take the life of all sorts of living things using lots of awesome looking guns. You have not just one, but many magazines in your grocery stores that are filled with pictures of awesome looking guns you can buy or admire them just as they are. Then, after all that, you pretend to be surprised when your dreams actually do come true and someone slaughters lots of people with awesome looking guns—just like they do on TV, in the movies, or in games. The world doesn't need gun control, it needs self-control. Stop giving the world the idea that all your problems with people you don't like or can't get along with, can be solved with awesome looking guns, that way people will stop believing that all their problems with other people can be solved with awesome looking guns. You can't preach gun control and then turn around and worship them.

So the question you need to ask yourself is, weren't the guns Adam Lanza picked out for his murders, awesome looking?